Manipulation techniques

The art of mind control and psychological manipulation. Get what you want, protect yourself and use manipulation in relationship. How to manage your emotions effectively.

Author James D. Mill

Table of Contents

Introduction

Manipulation refers to the act of regulating somebody for your benefit, often fraudulently. The art of manipulation does not have to necessarily involve making people act the way you want them to, but it rather entails causing them to want to react the way you desire them to.

There are several ways you can use to get people to proceed the way you desire or require them to. You have to know their true yearnings, then reverse this towards the goal you want to achieve. Manipulation is more of a psychological scheme since it aims at changing the thought process of an individual through indirect and underhanded tactics. If the manipulator advances his or her interests, then such tactics are considered as manipulative and devious.

The handier the person is to you, the more stress-free it is to manipulate them. In most cases, your romantic partners are the best people to use when testing your manipulation skills. Controlling someone, and if it feels like a bad word; persuading someone, involves making someone feel like it was their decision all along.

It has been established that men are easily manipulated through mastery and the individuality accompanying improvement since all they want is perfectionism. On the other hand, women tend to have balanced life relationships with their families and friends. Therefore, overpowering influences on precise interactions create a scorching longing to bring it up. In simple terms, this means that while women lean towards balance, men lean towards their emphasis on fastidiousness.

When manipulating someone, most individuals opt for the short term, but the real art of manipulation entails being affectionate about the long-term game. You need to be patient and make the persuasion look natural just like a professional, and the persuasiveness should flow without requiring loads of efforts. This forbearance helps in incapacitating the intellectual barriers that eventually helps you to have the right mindset.

There are several factors that motivate people to opt for manipulations. Some of them include (though are not limited to):

- The want to improve someone's gains and goals at the cost of others.

- A strong feeling of wanting to be the most powerful and superior, especially in relationships, and experience being in control. This entails wishing to raise the self-esteem of other people due to the power you have.

- Having covert or criminal agendas. This mostly results in financial manipulation, more so if the victim is defenseless, as in the case of the elderly.

- Lack of identification with underlying feelings; thus having a commitment phobia. A manipulator ends up manipulating unconsciously and convinces themselves on the baselessness of the emotions.

Chapter 1 What Is Manipulation And How Does It Work?

"The key to victory lies more in manipulation and cooperation than in exceptional personal skills" - Yuval Noah Harari

Manipulation is a form of social influence which uses indirect, underhanded, and deceptive tactics to change people's perceptions and their resultant behavior. Usually, the end goal is to advance the interests of the person who initiates the manipulation. In many cases, manipulation happens at the expense of the person that is being manipulated; they may be emotionally, mentally, or physically harmed, or they may end up taking actions that are against their own best interests.

It's important to note that social influence is not inherently bad; one person can use manipulation techniques for the good of the person he or she is manipulating. For example, your family members or friends can use social influence and manipulation to get you to do something for your own good. The people who mean you well might manipulate you as a way of helping you deal with certain challenges or to help you make the right decisions.

However, in this book, we won't focus on the garden-variety harmless forms of social influence. We are more interested in the kind of manipulation that is done with malicious intentions. This is the kind of manipulation that disregards a person's right to accept or reject influence. It is coercive in nature; when the person being targeted tries to push against it, this kind of manipulation gets more sophisticated, and the end goal is to negate the person's will to assert for themselves.

How Manipulation Works

There are several psychological theories that explain how successful manipulation works. The first and perhaps the most universally accepted theory is one that was put forth by renowned psychologist and author, George Simon. He analyzed the concept of manipulation from the point of view of the manipulator, and he can up with a pattern of behavior that sums up every manipulation scenario. According to Simon, there are three main things that are involved in psychological manipulation.

First, the manipulator approaches the target by concealing his or her aggressive intentions. Here, the manipulator seeks to endear himself to his target without revealing the fact that his ultimate plan is to manipulate him or her. The manipulator accomplishes this by modifying his behavior and presenting himself as a good-natured and friendly individual, one who relates well with the target.

Secondly, the manipulator will take time to know the victim. The purpose of this is to get to understand the psychological vulnerabilities that the victim may have so as to figure out which manipulation tactic will be the most effective when he ultimately decides to deploy them.

Depending on the scenario, and the complexity of the manipulation technique, this stage may take anywhere between a few minutes to several years. For example, when a stranger targets you, he may take only a couple of minutes to "size you up" but when your partner or colleague seeks to manipulate you, he or she may spend months or even years trying to understand how your mind works.

The success of this second step depends on how well the first step is executed. If the manipulator successfully hides his intentions from you, he is in a better position to learn your weaknesses because you will instill some level of trust in him, and he will use that trust to get you to let down your guard and to reveal your vulnerabilities to him.

Thirdly, having collected enough information to act upon, the manipulator will deploy a manipulation technique of his choosing. For this to work, the manipulator needs to be able to marshal a sufficient level of ruthlessness; this means that the manipulation technique chosen will depend on what the manipulator can stomach. A manipulator with a conscience may try to use methods that are less harmful to manipulate you. One that completely lacks a conscious may use extreme methods to take advantage of you. Either way, manipulative people are willing to let harm befall their victims, and to them, the resultant outcome (which is usually in their favor) justifies the harm they cause.

Simon's theory of manipulation teaches us the general approach that manipulators use to get what they want from their victims, but it also points out something extremely important: Manipulation works, not just because of the actions of the manipulator, but also because of the reactions of the victims.

In the first step, the manipulator misrepresents himself to the victim: If the victim is able to see through the veil that the manipulator is wearing, the manipulation won't be successful. In the second step, the manipulator collects information about victims to learn about his or her vulnerabilities. The victim can be may be able to stop the manipulation at this stage by treating the manipulator's prying nature with a bit of suspicion. In the third stage, the manipulator uses coercive or underhanded techniques to get what he wants from the victim. Even in this stage, the victim may have certain choices on how to react to the manipulator's machinations.

The point here is that when it comes to manipulation, it takes two to tango. By understanding both the victim's and the manipulator's psychology, it's possible to figure out how you can avoid falling victim to other people's manipulation, and it can also help you become more conscientious so that you don't unknowingly use manipulation techniques on other people around you.

Let's look at the vulnerabilities that manipulators like to exploit in their victims.

The first and most prevalent vulnerability is the need to please others. We all have this need to some extent; we seek to please the people in our lives as well as total strangers. This is technically a positive quality that helps us coexist in our societies, but to manipulators, it's a weapon that can be used against you.

Many of us are willing to endure certain levels of discomfort just to make other people feel happy; we feel a certain sense of obligation towards one another, and that's just human nature. The closer we are to certain people, the greater the need to please them. For example, the need to please your friend is higher than your need to please a stranger.

Manipulators understand this, and they use it against their victims all the time. If a manipulator wants to get something big out of you, he will first take the time to get closer to you, not just to get to know your vulnerability, but also to increase the sense of obligation you feel towards him.

The second vulnerability is the need for approval and acceptance. Again, as social beings, we all have an innate desire to feel accepted. We want people to love us, to think of us as members of their groups, and to choose us over other people. This feeling can be addictive, and it can give other people (especially manipulative ones) a lot of power over us. The vast majority of manipulation victims are people who have close personal relationships with the manipulators; in other words, they have an emotional need to gain the acceptance or approval of the manipulator. The remaining manipulation victims can be manipulated because they want to be a part of something (a group, a social class, etc.).

The third vulnerability that manipulators like to exploit is what psychologists refer to as "emetophobia" (which is the fear of negative emotions). To some extent, we are all afraid of negative emotions; we will do lots of things to avoid feeling angry, afraid, stressed, frustrated, and worried, etc. We want to lead happy and fulfilled lives, and anything that makes us feel "bad" is a threat to that sense of fulfillment. So, in many cases, we will do what manipulators want if it serves to alleviate that "bad" feeling. Manipulators know this, and they use negative emotions against us all the time.

The fourth vulnerability is the lack of assertiveness. Assertiveness is a very rare quality; even people who you may generally consider to be assertive are likely to cave in if manipulators push hard enough. Even when you are willing to stand your ground and to say "No," manipulators can be very persistent, and in the end, they can wear you out.

The fifth vulnerability is the lack of a strong sense of identity. Having a strong sense of identity means having clear personal boundaries, and understanding one's own values. Unfortunately, these qualities aren't so strong in most of us, and that leaves us open to manipulation. Manipulators succeed by pushing our boundaries little by little, making them blurry, and then taking control of our identities.

Finally, having an external locus of control, and having a low level of self-reliance are also key vulnerabilities that manipulators love to exploit. When you have an external locus of control, it means that your identity and your sense of self are external to you. It means you view yourself through other people's eyes. It means that you are extrinsically motivated. When you have low self-reliance, it means you depend on other people for sustenance and for emotional stability. It means that if support systems in your life are taken away, you can easily find yourself leaning on a manipulator, which leaves you at his mercy.

Chapter 2 Historical Background

"Manipulation, sloganizing, depositing, regimentation, and prescription cannot be components of revolutionary praxis, precisely because they are the components of the praxis of domination" - Paulo Freire

Manipulation has existed with man since the earliest civilizations. An ever-present yet background behavior that people will use to benefit themselves. Usually for the pettiest of reasons. But some have used manipulation for the attainment of great power such as the Roman Emperors who manipulated for the power over millions, to politicians today saying what we want to hear. All the way down to the lover quarreling in their relationship.

This begs the question of why, why someone would use social subterfuge for anything. Well, look at the people I mentioned prior they all have one thing in common. Power. They manipulated for the sake of power, and that power helped them accomplish many great things. Consider the modern corporate world. If you want to get ahead easily, you're going to do what is called by many individuals as "Playing the Game." Simply put you'll act the way your superiors want to act; you'll go out of your way to endear yourself to them. While at the same you prove that you are a more qualified employee for that opening you want to attain. Manipulation can have its roots in the earliest of human civilizations. This is simply because it works. You yourself manipulate and do not even realize it. Let's take this theoretical for example your good friends with someone and have helped them with difficult tasks before.

Can Manipulation be a Good Thing?

Well, now you need help moving, your most likely to go and try to call a close friend or family member because you know rather it be subconsciously or consciously that they will almost certainly help you. Simply by virtue of prior interactions you have had with them, interactions where you have helped them. So, as a result of this setup, you'll both be amicable to helping one another. Well, simply put that is manipulation because you recognize that the individuals you have asked for help from have asked you for help in the past. Hence this arrangement appears natural within the confines of this friendship, but it is still a form of manipulation, nonetheless.

This is also the odd part of manipulation; we use it so often in our daily lives to get things in what we think is a friendly way that benefits both parties in that they both feel good in the end. We end up becoming oblivious to the insidious side of manipulation to where the people using these tactics on us don't have anything for us to gain. They just want us to be manipulated into believing what they are offering counts as some kind of gain.

All of these behaviors are used in politics still today. A famous book by an Italian by the name of Niccolò Machiavelli written in Florence many hundreds of years ago who's simple premise is that it makes sense to manipulate in the fact that they would do the same to you had the tables been turned. His ideas help further cement these kinds of behaviors and activities as normal and acceptable. And as a result, many despotic world leaders began to cling to them, believing that it would hopefully provide them with power in the name of the people.

Concluding this point I would also like to point out the fact that some individuals who engage in manipulation are simply just mentally ill, and as a result of that, their manipulative behavior is stemming from a place of hurt, because in a place of hurt you are incapable of thinking rationally of your actions and the consequences that they may have on other people.

These people who use emotional manipulation as a defense mechanism oftentimes, do it because it is the only mechanism of psychological defense, they grew up knowing. These individuals with mental illness, for the most part, intend no malicious intent or are even mean at heart, but their behavior and activity they engage in can create that appearance. That still means don't go out of your way to try to help people like this such as boyfriends or girlfriends.

Romantic manipulation is by far the worst form that occurs and yet most common. Due to how it shatters trust barriers and bonds. So, in future encounters with manipulators, it is important for you to remember these things as they will help guide you in future encounters with manipulators since you now understand some of their storied histories.

We can begin to look at manipulation as it occurs now in the 21st century. Most of today's manipulation honestly occurs in something as simple as social media. What I am saying by this is people can manipulate and covertly trick us into thinking they live these blessed lives when, in reality, they don't. They show us only what looks good and what gets like. In a way manipulation has gone from the background to the foreground. It has moved into our everyday lives with things like "fake news" and internet links that are designed to sound enticing yet simply accomplish nothing more than selling an ad.

This why it is important as ever to understand manipulation, given how often it occurs in this fast-paced world of ours. This may sound devious, but manipulation can also be used to accomplish great things that benefit everyone, such as Gandhi's hunger strikes and other forms of peaceful negotiation. Concluding on the history of manipulation, just remember it has always been with us and always will be with us. It will just change forms over time.

Knowledge is the power

Knowledge is power, and you the reader knowing how people manipulate, the background on it, and why it happens, are now much better equipped to deal with manipulation when you encounter it in your day to life. But heed these last words because when looking at the history of manipulation do not always focus on the negative sometimes manipulation has accomplished great things and even saved lives.

As has been the case in things such as diplomacy. Think of it this way when you are arguing with a potential foe. It makes more sense to lie to them and tell them what they want to hear. Because if there are potentially millions of lives at stake, then why would you want to risk anything but an absolute success.

This may sound malevolent, but the fact of the matter is that sometimes, a bit of dishonesty needs to be used to allow honest virtues to thrive.

Finally, manipulation can also be used for good if you are a salesperson. The kind of manipulation used in sales as you will read further into this book. Tends to not be overt, it leans more on the subtle side of things as a result of how it functions and what the end goal of it is. To simply sell things, so remember while manipulation can look bad on the surface, it is what the end goal is that truly matters.

So now that we have covered the history of manipulation. You were probably left wondering why I mentioned manipulation can be used for good and how it may not perhaps always be bad. I used a prior summary to explain this, but now I would like to go into more depth about the matter. See the big issue with using manipulative tactics for good. Is the negative connotation manipulation carries with it as a word? When you hear it used to refer to someone or an organization in conversation, you're most likely going to assume something nefarious regarding them.

This is simply false!

Take the example of spies during World War II, who helped defeat the Nazis, their whole job was based on manipulation, but it was for a good cause – to save lives!

The spies had to lie and play a part, while also manipulating a target to get exactly what they need. The sad truth is that manipulation may, in some situations, be unavoidable – and we can't fool ourselves into thinking that good manipulation does not exist.   Imagine if you have bills to pay and work at a car dealership, well "sales tactics" are really manipulation.

Sales tactics are used to create an emotional and economic incentive for a potential customer even though, for the most part, they're probably false. But in this case, both parties win. From the perspective of the car salesperson they have now made a sale and can feed their families and themselves.

From the customer's outlook, they now believe they have earned a great deal on an expensive car and have somehow found someone who gives them exactly what they want in a product, thus giving them a sense of happiness. While on the surface, this is most definitely manipulation, it is something you could consider positive, given both parties win in their minds.

There is importance in knowing when it's healthy to use manipulation to defend yourself is as equally important. Take, for instance, you suddenly start noticing your significant other always putting you on the spot or always playing the victim in every single situation.

Then it dawns on you they're a covert manipulator. Well, if you know manipulation tactics on your own, you can spot them in relationships and by virtue of understanding their use. You can completely avoid them in individuals who may potentially act like this. In situations like these your using manipulation out of peer necessity. For whatever reason, you may need someone to get talked out or into something, so you don't get harmed. Funnily enough using manipulation tactics against police officers to avoid a traffic stop is a good example of this.

You are doing that simply because it is one of your only choices, so you don't get hit with a large fine. If you play on their emotions by claiming your violation for speeding was to visit a sick family member then, yes, it's outright manipulation.

More importantly, though, it saved you economically. I am sure this sounds bad, but how many of us have ever found ourselves in a situation where we may face a possible traffic ticket and have thought to ourselves that we would do anything to get out of it. Well, sometimes manipulation, when used right, is the best way possible to do that.

Manipulation is a Part of Human History

Looking at history, we will see that some of our most loved historical figures practiced manipulation. During the founding of the United States, our founding fathers had to use socio-political manipulation to help set a revolution in motion. By first using various economic manipulation tactics on the other colonies and colonists that joining their cause would benefit them more than say the British. Secondly, among each other many political games had to be played, all using subterfuge and manipulation to help get the right people in place to lead the country.

Manipulation had to be used in its persuasive form here so that the right person could get the right backing. This was not evil nor bad; it showed how the covert tactic of playing into a willing pawns card could allow for everyone involved to win. Imagine, too, that they had to manipulate the British for quite a while before things truly were sent into emotion. They had to manipulate them into trusting and believing them. These same kinds of manipulative games have been used for good by many great figures in history to simply manipulate their opposition into doing what is right.

Think of the rallies and marches during the civil rights movement. It did so much good by manipulating and playing on people's emotions and wants for a just society. This is not malicious manipulation, but more so an evil required to enact great change in this world.

Knowing that manipulation is not always an evil wantonly committed for evil makes it much easier to understand the kind of tactics people will use. In a big part complimenting and persuading someone through charisma is, in a sense, manipulation. You are telling them what they want to hear whether it compliments or being a shoulder to cry on for someone.

Almost every friendship that is healthy has this give and take. For a large part, these are simple altruistic forms of manipulation that allow and help both sides win and accomplish a goal of theirs. Charisma and persuasion two topics I mentioned earlier. Persuasion and charisma are the simplest forms of human manipulation.

Manipulators work by making someone come across as if they are the type of person who loves and cares about you and would drop anything if need be to help you with something. This glib or charm is a manipulative tactic that one could use for themselves to try and gain friends. Once again, there is nothing wrong with this; its more in line with gaming the system. You are putting on a front that people want, and as a result of this, they then become drawn to you easier and wish to spend time with you or do stuff to you.

This is a simple day to day manipulation that we all do – whether we realize it or not. This type of manipulation on a social scale is not for harm, but for companionship. Have you ever heard the expression "a little white lie"? The issue is that the word makes manipulation sound bad and evil. But the truth is that by doing simple things that social charmer does, like mirroring body language, buying someone food, or always asking about their interests and ignoring yours is basic human interaction. You can get people to trust you and even help you get ahead in life, especially if this kind of interaction is taking place in the social world.

Manipulation and Success

You could argue that to a certain degree without some powerful people in society who used manipulation to get their way to the top, the world would fall apart. Maybe we would not be so successful. This kind of manipulation is far more different than the much more sinister mind manipulation. It is simple to understand the term mental manipulation. Simply put, mental manipulation occurs with the nefarious act of playing mind games, such as making you feel guilty for not buying or doing something, getting you to question your own judgment.

This covert manipulative behavior can become so common that we oftentimes don't recognize it until it is too late by which point, we have befallen the consequences of said manipulation. Avoiding these consequences is a great thing to be capable of doing. But it can be hard to avoid if you are not sure what you are avoiding. Well, that is why it is good to know what mental manipulation is due to its subtlety. It is this type of manipulation – mental manipulation – which is perhaps the most common form of manipulation you will encounter in your day to day life.

Mental manipulation shows its face a lot in relationships with friends or other people you care about. As a result, the people who do this are very good at it and hide it well. Besides being such a common form of manipulation people will use, it is important to realize that there are many varieties of mental manipulation to which you could easily find yourself as a victim.

Consider times when you are speaking with a group of friends, and one person tries to make you feel guilty due to you making a choice to not buy them an extremely expensive gift for their birthday. They then might try mental manipulation to get you to fall for the trap of "oh well, I have done all these things for you; do you not think it is fair if you get me xyz."

Behavior like this is where manipulation becomes evil and unacceptable. This is not trying to sway someone over to your side of thinking for a good reason or trying to survive in a time of crisis. This narcissistic person is using manipulation to hurt people, and that is never acceptable.

Understanding the subtle moral differences in manipulation makes it easier for you to appreciate how to learn about different manipulative tactics as a whole and how you yourself can go about defending from and using them as well as giving you the useful ability of knowing how to avoid people who could potentially try and manipulate you in person, this includes the media and everything else we see. Since they all use manipulation tactics, understanding this is half the battle.

Chapter 3 Manipulation and the Question of Morality

"The purpose of morality is to teach you, not to suffer and die, but to enjoy yourself and live" - Ayn Rand

If you are reading this book, it means that you might be on the fence about, or totally on the side of manipulation. Most people will clutch their pearls when they notice someone reading a guide on manipulation. Expect this same reaction from the people around you. The question of whether manipulation is moral or immoral is one that is not likely to be answered anytime soon. There are a lot of grey areas to be considered. For instance, what is the manipulation intended to achieve and who is the target? If you manipulate someone into donating to your favorite charity, does this still count as immoral? At the workplace, where do you draw the line between ethical and unethical manipulation, and who sets the rules for either?

There are some instances where manipulation has been used to harm other people. In such an instance, it is easy to say that a line has been crossed. But then again, while the moral compass is supposed to always point north, not everyone has this compass. Morality and immorality are subjective depending on various factors. That being said, there are instances where it is almost unanimously agreed that manipulation is a good thing. In such instances, nobody will bat an eyelid when persistent persuasion is being used to achieve a particular objective.

Since their inception, non-profit organizations and non-governmental organizations have relied upon the goodwill of donors to further their agenda. Getting people to give you their money is not an easy task. If you thought asking investors for capital is hard, try asking for money that will not have any monetary returns. It can definitely be an uphill task. Instead, what nonprofits have mastered is the art of persuading donors to give their money for the greater good of the world.

These nonprofits are very deliberate in approaching their donors. They know that people will give to causes that they are passionate about. As such, they have profiles of people they would like to approach which they crossmatch with the kind of work they do. It would be foolish and a waste of time for a nonprofit to approach a donor who has no interest in the particular field of operation of the nonprofit. Once the befitting donor has been identified, the next step is to persuade them to make a donation, and potentially a long-standing contribution. Remember the concept of the idealized self-image? Now, the trick is to appeal to the image the person has of themselves: that they are a giving person and are always engaged in altruistic acts for the greater good of the world and the less fortunate. Some people like to refer to this as the massaging of an ego.

The donor now has an expectation to live up to. He has this non-profit organization that is engaged in something that he cares about, and the non-profit thinks the world of him. Sooner than later, there will be a check addressed to the said organization. The donor will feel so good about himself and will continue making donations for as long as he can; after all, he is a kind and giving person. In the meantime, the donations are used to help important causes, and the world is a better place as a result.

Manipulation against the backdrop of capitalism is yet another area that is quite grey. For instance, if you make a product and manipulate people into thinking that is worth more than it actually is, and they pay for it, does that make you a bad person? Think of all the overpriced items in this world and the people spending their hard-earned money to pay for them. Who is at fault here? Is anybody really at fault? While a shopper spends $1000 on a handbag that ideally should cost less, a struggling sales assistant gets a reprieve in the form of sales commission. Does the manipulation equation balance out in this case?

Employees in the workplace have different levels of motivation. Some employees come to work because they are passionate about what they do. Some only show up because they have bills to pay. There are yet others who have yet to figure out why they keep showing up even though they mentally checked out months ago. As a manager, how effective is it to use direct and upfront means to motivate each and every employee that works under you? Sometimes you have to resort to manipulation. It gets the job done faster.

The decision of where morality meets manipulation is indeed a very personal one. If you want to benefit fully from this book, you must make that decision very early on. Considering that you have read this book so far (and most of the techniques described herein are humane), you are likely to be interested in going through with it. However, choosing to adopt manipulation in your daily life is not the same as knowing how to deal with the consequences. If telling a single lie keeps you awake at night, you'll probably not have a very easy time manipulating people. Keep this in mind but remember too that what might seem impossible at first might become easier as you get used to it. You might get better at telling bigger lies if you practice with some little fibs.

At the same time, you need to be able to draw the line as far as deciding who is a target for your manipulation and who is not. If you have a dear and loving relationship with your parents, you might want to let it remain as so and keep the manipulation out of the family home. Being outed as a manipulator or liar could very easily cost you the opportunity to enjoy a loving relationship with our family members. Again, this is all subjective. If family is not important to you, you are at liberty to manipulate them into giving you what you want.

The morality of manipulation really is a personal question that requires a personal answer.

Why Manipulation is Important in Your Life

Manipulation matters in your life, whether you believe in it or not, and whether you are conflicted by the morality of it or not. This is why manipulation is essential if you are hoping to survive your current circumstances:

- *It gives you back the power in your life. Having been a pawn in the manipulation games of individuals, corporates and even governments, you can take back ownership of your life by becoming manipulative. Consider it your subtle and small-scale rebellion against the system.*

- *It makes you more productive. Instead of sitting and waiting for things to happen, you can go out and make them happen. Life does not give you everything you want on a silver platter. Life can indeed be very unfair is you are constantly playing nice and warming the bench. Be one of the key players by getting people to meet your demands.*

- *It makes you feel better about yourself. Imagine being able to get anything that you wanted. How would that make you feel? Confident? Most likely. After years of hearing no, it would feel pretty great to hear yes on a more regular basis.*

- *It helps you create a network of 'friends' that you can rely on to solve your problems. Social and professional networks always come in handy. After all, man cannot exist in isolation. When manipulating people, you will often present yourself as a trustworthy friend who can be called upon in business and personal matters. This is important for your own advancement.*

- *Manipulation allows you to do less legwork. Imagine being able to achieve your dreams without getting exhausted? Dreamy, right? Right. If you manipulate the right people into being your helpers, you can accomplish all your goals without getting worn out.*

- *Being manipulative protects you from manipulation. You already know what tactics to look out for, and nobody will be able to outwit you unless you let them win on purpose.*

- *The world is a cruel place that is not intended for softies and pushovers. Nobody said that playing fair was going to get you the things that you want. Understanding and applying manipulation techniques in your life allows you to be properly prepared to survive in the harsh environment of a majorly capitalistic world.*

- *Manipulative people are often charming and leave smiles on the faces of the people they interact with. Essentially, being manipulative might help you to make other people happier. Yes, their joy might be short-lived, but it will be joy all the same. And remember, if you play your cards right, you will never have to worry about their joy is short-lived mainly because they will never catch onto you.*

- *By learning how to be manipulative, you will be joining in the ranks of great men and women who learned how to be manipulative years ago and used it to their advantage. There is no pushover that has ever made it to the history books. The people who capture the hearts and minds of historians have one thing in common: they know what they want, and they use all means at their disposal, manipulation included, to achieve this.*

- *Manipulation forces you to use your brain all the time. All your interactions have to be well processed by your mind, and every move that you make must be strategic. It is like being in an exciting and never-ending game of chess. This sharpens your brain, and you can use this brain power to better other areas in your life.*

Chapter 4 Managing Situations And Emotions

"The first and simplest emotion which we discover in the human mind, is curiosity" - Edmund Burke

When trying to influence, persuade, or manipulate someone, being able to read their emotions is vital to your success. They will allow you to gauge how well your efforts are going or how badly. After all, our emotions have a huge influence on the decisions we make and the actions we take, which makes understanding your subject's emotions vital to your efforts.

Before you can read emotions, you need to understand what they comprise. Let us begin by looking at your own emotions. They are made up of three important components:

- The subjective component. This is how you, personally, experience the emotion. It has nothing to do with how others see it.

- The physiological component. This is how your body reacts to the emotion. Does your heart race? Do your palms sweat?

- The expressive component. This is how you behave in response to the emotion. Do you cry, smile, laugh, cringe? Do you throw your arms around your partner and kiss them?

The Role of Emotions

Emotions generally play four roles. They motivate, they help us survive, they help us make decisions, and they help us communicate. Without them, day to day life would be nearly impossible.

Motivation

Imagine that you are faced with a very tight deadline at work, but you are under a lot of pressure to get the project done on time. Perhaps a major contract is riding on your actions over the next few hours. Maybe your job is riding on it. How would you feel? Most of us would feel particularly anxious, especially if our livelihood was in the balance. As a result of that anxiety, you would be more likely to put in extra hours, start the project early, even get help from coworkers. You had an emotional response, anxiety, and you took action to get the job done and alleviate that anxiety. On the positive side, your love for your girlfriend could make you feel pressured to propose marriage. You could also seek out activities and experiences that induce positive emotions like happiness or excitement, and avoid those that induce feelings of sadness or boredom.

Survival

Charles Darwin, the author of On the Origin of Species, held that emotions were evolutionary adaptations that fostered survival and reproduction in both humans and animals. They motivate us to act quickly and take actions that will maximize our chances of survival and success. Anger leads us to confrontation, while fear induces us to flee a threat. Lust makes us seek out a mate; love makes us take care of the people close to us.

Decision-making

Emotions play a major role in the decisions we make, from what movie we watch after work to what we have for dinner to who we vote for at election time. Each one has an emotional component that informs the choices we make, even those that we truly believe are purely rational and logical. In fact, research shows that brain damage affecting the areas of the brain that control emotions is linked to a markedly decreased ability to make good decisions.

Communication

Emotions help us to understand others and to be understood. Our emotions offer important clues to those communicating with us as to how we are feeling. Sometimes this is done with facial expressions, sometimes with body language, and sometimes with explicit statements. This provides a point of understanding and an opportunity to take action in response to a given situation.

Understanding Emotions in Others

Reading emotions in others is a function of your emotional intelligence. If you are going to be persuasive, influential, or even manipulative, improving your emotional intelligence will go a long way toward helping you reach your goals.

Universal Human Emotions

The first thing to do is to be able to recognize that there are two positive emotions and four negative ones. The positive ones are happiness and surprise. They reduce stress and improve mood. They also improve memory and awareness. The negative emotions are anger, fear, sadness, and disgust. They each increase stress, but they also help us to recognize and deal with threats and difficult situations. Each of these emotions is associated with a distinct set of behaviors, and to identify them in other people you need to learn to recognize those behaviors.

Facial Expressions

Now you are ready to start learning to read emotions. We will begin with facial expressions as they are an extremely important part of nonverbal communication. Just hearing a person's words without the benefit of seeing their facial expressions only gives you part of the message because words frequently do not match the emotions. You need to read the facial expression to know what the person you are speaking with is really feeling. It will help guide you through the conversation. Just remember that if you nail the emotion someone is feeling, you still do not know why they feel that way. If you are speaking with someone who seems upset or bored, they could be feeling that way for any number of reasons that have nothing to do with you.

Facial Expressions and Universal Emotions

There are seven facial expressions: surprise, fear, disgust, contempt, anger, sadness, and happiness. These expressions are universal across all cultures and are the same regardless of race, sex, country of origin. You could be from Paris trying to communicate with someone from the Amazon rainforest, and both of you would recognize these expressions. Get in front of a mirror and put in some time practicing each of them. Take your time and really explore them, and you will soon get much better at recognizing each of them in others.

Reading the Face

Once you have an idea about your own expressions, it is time to look at other people. Just remember, however, that these expressions are not necessarily automatic. As you can see in your own exercises, it is easy to manipulate your expression to appear one way when, in reality, you are feeling something very different. That is why you have to look at the whole person and listen to their voice. Here are some things to look for:

•   A genuine smile. Fake smiles you very few facial muscles, primarily those just around the mouth, while the genuine smile encompasses far more of the face with the corners of the mouth as well as the cheeks raised and the area around the eyes tightened into "crow's feet." These characteristics together point to a genuine smile.

•   Know the difference between happiness and sadness. People will often try to cover-up sadness by smiling. Again, look at the entire face. While a frown is a dead giveaway for sadness, look for a raising of the inner corners of the eyebrows and loose, drooping eyelids.

•   Know the difference between anger and disgust. Anger and disgust are easily confused because they are associated with similar facial expressions. For example, people tend to wrinkle their noses when they are disgusted, angry, or simply annoyed, so you need to look for other clues. Anger is usually expressed by pulling down the eyebrows, bulging the eyes and pursing the lips.

On the other hand, emotions like disgust, disdain or dislike can be seen in the raising of the upper lip and a simultaneous loosening of the lower lip, as well as furrowing of the brow, but not to the same extent as anger.

•	Recognize the difference between fear and surprise. Fear and surprise can be thought of as two sides of the same coin in that each of them activates an instinctual "fight or flight" response, whether or not it is a true threat. In both cases, the eyes go wide, which allows us to better see a threat coming. The difference is in the eyebrows, which rise in surprise as the jaw drops; and furrow in fear, with dilated pupils. Also, fear makes us open our mouths and tense our facial muscles.

Micro-expressions

Facial expressions that pass quickly are referred to as micro-expressions. They are there one moment and gone the next, and they are almost indiscernible unless you are looking for them. Have you ever had a feeling about someone that you just could not pin down? If so, you could be picking up on a micro-expression. Here are a few things to look for:

•	Eyebrows. Watching the eyebrows will tell you a great deal about what a person is feeling. Eyebrows can be:

•	Raised and arched, which shows surprise.

•	Lowered and knit together in anger.

•	Angled, with the inner corners drawn up, which shows sadness.

•	Eyes. As expressive as eyebrows are, they can't hold a candle to the eyes themselves. They can be:

•	Open wide to show surprise,

•	Intense and staring in a way that screams anger, or

•	Framed by wrinkles (crow's feet), a sign of happiness.

Note: Dilated pupils are an indication of either fear or lust, while rapid blinking is a definite sign of either a stress reaction or lying.

•	Mouth. Next, to the eyes, the mouth is the most expressive part of the face. There are a number of things you should look for, including:

•	An open mouth with a lowered jaw, which signals surprise.

•	A tense open mouth, which shows fear.

•	A sneer with a single corner of the mouth raised to show hatred.

•	Both corners raised in a smile of happiness.

•	Both corners are drawn down in a frown of sadness.

The mouth can signal other things as well, including:

•	Anxiety through lip biting.

- Distaste through pursed lips.

- Deceit by covering the mouth.

Vocal Tone

The next thing to consider is the vocal tone. While it does come into play as an emotional expression, it is not foolproof. This is because not all emotions are strongly expressed in the voice. Some of the weaker ones include happiness, sadness, fear, and friendliness. More than that, different emotions can be expressed with very similar tones. A tense voice can mean anger, for example, but it can also mean excitement.

Depending on the intensity, a whispery or soft tone is concordant with a number of positive emotions including lust, relaxation, contentment, and friendship; but it also could indicate either sadness or boredom. If the tone is breathier, the more likely it is to indicate fear, shyness, or nervousness.

General Behavior and Demeanor

Emotional displays often happen with the person being completely unaware of what they are doing. In fact, a person's general behavior and demeanor often speak volumes about how they are feeling. When you look at the person, to they seem open and friendly, or are they closed off, and reserved? Again, you do not know why they might be feeling the way they do, but these signs will give you a clue as to how to proceed.

• Look for nonverbal cues. These will help you read emotion but do not rely solely upon them as there is often a cultural, physical, or psychological component involved. You are looking for body movements, posture, and eye contact. Notice whether or not the person appears to be relaxed and animated, maintaining good eye contact and posture, and moving easily. If so, great; but a tense, stiff posture, especially if they stoop, fidget or make other displays of irritation or nervousness all indicate negative emotions. A relaxed, straight posture with easy movement shows comfort and openness, but too much movement, especially combined with a loud voice, indicates excitement or anger. On the other hand, stooped shoulders and crossed arms indicate things like extreme discomfort or defensiveness, while a refusal to make eye contact can indicate upset or guilt.

• Remember that body language is heavily influenced by culture, personality, and social situations. Italians, for example, use gestures when they speak, while in Japan, such gesturing could be considered rude. Another example is eye contact. In the United States and Europe, eye contact denotes attention and respect, but some Asian and African cultures see it as rude or aggressive.

• Notice body movement and posture. Posture and body movement will show both the emotion as well as its intensity. Hunched shoulders combined with a forward-leaning posture denotes intense anger, while a more backward-leaning stance indicates panic or fear. We see an air of confidence in a straight posture with the shoulders back and head held high, but hunched shoulders or a pronounced forward slump indicates boredom, nervousness, or a need for sympathy. Hands at the side or in the pockets tend to indicate sadness, while annoyance or irritation is displayed with one arm at the side or hand on the hip, and the other hand gesturing, either pointing or with the palm flat. Hands behind the back indicate indifference. In regard to legs and feet, shaking legs or tapping toes can indicate anxiety, annoyance or impatience. They could also mean nothing at all.

•	Notice signs of "fight or flight" reaction. When we are surprised or threatened, we experience a stress reaction that includes widened pupils, faster breathing, sweating, and heart palpitations. Sweaty palms or armpits, flushed complexion, and shaking hands all indicate stress, anxiety, or nervousness. Men react to stress and upset by becoming aggressive, angry, and/or frustrated, while women react by being more interactive, seeking help, and discussing their situation. That's not everyone, mind you, as there are those whose reaction to stress and upset is to withdraw, some describe it as "going underground."

Look to Your Own Reactions

Emotions are contagious, passing easily from one person to another. We have all experienced our mood changing as a result of someone else's emotion. You can use this to recognize emotions in others by taking note of your own reaction, the facial expression, tone, and body language you adopt in answer to someone else's emotions.

Emotion and Health

There is a direct connection between physical health and emotions. Stress and depression, for example, can leave you feeling sick and tired all the time with headaches, stomach issues, pain, and a host of other physical symptoms. They can also lead to alterations in eating habits as well as addictions to alcohol and/or drugs.

Improving Your Emotional Intelligence

You can develop and improve your emotional intelligence over time by observing your own emotions and, when looking at other people, applying what you have learned about your emotions to theirs. Begin by learning the four areas of emotional intelligence:

1.   See and recognize your own emotions and the emotions of others;

2.   Use what you have perceived in yourself and others as a basis to think about what is happening;

3.   Learn the true importance of the role these emotions play and their meaning; and

4.   Learn how to control your own emotional reactions and help others do likewise.

Since there is really no app for this, here are some strategies you can use to improve your emotional intelligence starting right now. They include:

•	Work on your ability to read facial expressions and body language. It will require that you put the cellphone down and actually engage in verbal, in-person dialog every day.

•	Face your own uncomfortable or negative feelings, as well as those you see in others. Understand that these are valid feelings and that there is a reason you are experiencing them. You just need to figure out why and then counteract them with positive emotions.

•	Consider your health and bodily reactions. Your emotions and your body are linked, so pay attention to how it reacts when you are happy, sad, excited, and so on.

•	Keep an Emotions Journal. Here you are to write down how you are feeling and record your activity at the time of the feeling as well as the thoughts you have that go along with those emotions. Include anything that you deem relevant. The key is to understand the connection between emotions, actions, and thoughts.

•	Get an Emotion Reading from some close to you, a friend or family member that you trust. Having a different perspective is often quite useful and insightful, and the answers you get may be both interesting and unexpected.

When All Else Fails, Just Ask

There is nothing wrong with simply asking someone how they are feeling. Try to speak to them alone; it will help them to open up to you, which may be difficult if they are in a group setting.

However, the other person might also lie and tell you that everything is fine when it really isn't. That is not uncommon, but it is also not the end of the world. Their response when you ask can tell you a lot by giving you a chance to examine their non-verbal expressions as well as how they respond to you. Low tones and slow speech could indicate sadness, while higher tones and more rapid speech can indicate excitement or upset. Remember, context is important when trying to decipher the meanings behind these emotional expressions.

Gauging Your Influence

As you go through and practice these strategies of persuasion and influence, the most common question is this: How do I know it is working, and if it is working, by how much? One way is to simply count the number of times you get your way. That will not give you the whole story, though. You also need to consider the demeanor of the person you have influenced. Did they act or change willingly, or did they do it resentfully, just to get rid of you? If that is the case, then you cannot really count it as a win. When you convert someone to your way of thinking or get them to do something for you, they should do it willingly. Once you start getting that, you know your efforts have risen above mere nagging.

Another way of judging your influence has less to do with how many people do what you want them to do, and more to do with how you affect them. The key to judging your influence over others by this method is to see how others influence you. Ask yourself, how have I been influenced by the people I met today? How many made me happy? How many angered me? How many saddened me? How many excited me? Think back to each of these encounters and jot down some notes describing how you were feeling before the encounter and how you felt after. Really get in touch with how others make you feel throughout the day.

Now, turn the tables and contemplate how you have affected the people around you all day. What sort of influence have you exerted on others? The more aware you become of the influence you have, the quicker you will understand how effectively you influence them.

In the next chapter, we will dig into one of the most popular methods of manipulation and influence, Neuro-Linguistic Programming.

Chapter 5 Emotional Manipulation

"The experience of life consists of the experience which the spirit has of itself in matter and as matter, in mind and as mind, in emotion, as emotion, etc" - Franz Kafka

When it comes to emotional manipulation, there are two main categories, covert and overt.

Covert emotional manipulation includes all of the invisible manipulation techniques. These emotional attacks by the manipulator can't be seen until it all compounds and create a problem. These techniques are intentional and the manipulator will make sure that they are well prepared to harm their victim in a psychological way.

These attacks leave you thinking that everything happened accidentally, but the abuser knows exactly what is going on. The extreme covert manipulator is often referred to as narcissists or psychopaths. They follow their own systematic emotional attack in order to break their victim's confidence and control their world. This leaves their victim as their puppet without the victim realizing anything.

When it comes to cover manipulation, the abuser creates a twisted reality. This misguided view brainwashes you and messed with your ability to make the right decisions. The abuser is then able to guide you as they please.

Overt emotional manipulation includes the techniques that the victim notices and experiences. These fall into the sexual, verbal, and physical abuse categories. These are situations where you have a better chance of knowing that you are being manipulated, but there are some who still don't realize what is happening.

Cover and over manipulations should be on your watch list. As the book progresses, you will learn ways to deal with them.

We're going to take a stroll through some different behaviors of an emotional manipulator. Then we will look at the different types of manipulators. This is by no means an exhaustive list of behaviors, but it will help you in spotting the manipulative person.

1.   Home court

The manipulative person will often insist on meeting in areas that they consider "home." These are areas where they can exercise more control and dominance. This could be their car, home, office, or other spaces that they are familiar with and you aren't.

1.   You speak first to give them a baseline of your weaknesses

A lot of salespeople will use the tactic when they are trying to sell you something. By asking probing and general questions, they are able to create a baseline about your behavior and the way you think. They can then use this to evaluate your weaknesses and strengths. This hidden agenda type questioning occurs often in the workplace and in romantic relationships.

1.   Too many statistics and facts

Some manipulators like to be an "intellectual bully" by presuming that they are the expert and are more knowledgeable in certain areas. They try to take advantage of people by imposing alleged statistics, facts, and other forms of data that you don't know much about. This often happens in financial situations and sales, and in professional negotiations and discussions, and sometimes in relational and social arguments. By exacting expert power over their victim, the manipulator hopes to push their agenda on your in a more convincing manner. Some manipulators will do this for no other reason than to feel intellectually superior over another.

1.   They overwhelm you with red tape

A lot of manipulators will use committees, laws, procedures, paperwork, and other roadblocks to keep their power and position while also making your life difficult. They often do this to delay fact-finding, hide weaknesses and flaws, and evade questioning.

1.   Negative surprises

There are some people who will use negative surprises to knock their victim off balance and gain an emotional advantage. This could be low balling during negotiations, to suddenly professing that they won't be able to deliver in some way. This unexpected negative information typically happens without warning, so you won't have much time to prepare and counter what they say. They may end up asking for additional concessions for you.

Types of Manipulators

There are several types of manipulators that you can come across that have a particular technique they like to use. That's not to say that it is the only technique they use, but it is their favorite.

1.   The Adaptable One

"I observe those around me before I choose my manipulation tactics."

These are the most dangerous manipulators. They have mastered all of the techniques in order to form their self to any situation. They adapt and change according to the personality of their victims. They use a mixture of techniques to come up with the perfect blend of manipulation that you can't get out of. Even if they end up failing, they will never stop. They learn and try different tactics to gain better control over others. They get a thrill when people try to resist their manipulation. They try to find strong personalities just to test their skills.

1.   The Intimidator

"You won't like it if I get mad."

These manipulators use intimidation to get what they want. The demand things and bully people to get it. They want to be the answer to the how, why, what, and when of their victims. Everything you do or say has to go along with their plan. These manipulators will often use their physical features to bully. In fact, a lot of them won't shy away from using physical abuse to intimidate their victims.

The intimidator doesn't have to be just physically strong people. There are some who use their intelligence as a way to intimidate others. If you disagree with them, they will show you "evidence" that they are better than you.

1.   The Charming One

"I'm pretty, so you have to give me what I want."

These manipulators charm you into a relationship and then enact control over you. Their attractiveness becomes their weapon. They are very superficial and likely view their self as more attractive than they really are. They must be the favorite person in your life. Their flirtiness and sexual triggers are what helps them lure in their victims. They want people to react in a positive way to their flirtatious nature. They love causing tension among friends and family.

They are always on the lookout for new partners. They make sure they have a strong connection with their current partner, but they are always on the lookout for potential partners. They don't follow traditional relationship structures. In fact, if families and friendships break up, it makes them feel empowered.

1.   The Denier

"I'm the good one and you are the bad one."

These manipulators are full of ego, so much so that they deny their own actions. They don't understand their flaws and project these on their victims. They see their faults but think that everybody else in the world has them. They blame their victims and will sometimes try to include others in their blame game. Their stubbornness doesn't allow them to realize the flaws they have. They truly believe everything they say and do is right.

1.   The Truth Twister

"Sorry, but I think I misunderstood what you said."

These manipulators gain control over their victims through lies, exaggerations, and half-truths. They will carefully change their victim's words and will turn them into rumors. If they are exposed, they will deny and apologize with something like, "I misunderstood what you said." They want to feel superior in their group, even when it is undeserved. They are friendly by nature, which allows them to blend in with others.

1.   The Wrong Well-Wisher

"I am your own true friend. Everybody else just wants to use you for your good nature."

Hiding the complete story, lying, and other techniques are a part of this manipulators arsenal. They want to isolate you from others by feeing your lies. They also present themselves as the only well-wisher in your life. Creating an alliance with you is how they live their life. Their friendliness keeps you from spotting their true intentions. Then, once they have gained complete control, they start spreading rumors and serve as the only source of information for their victim. This leaves the victim angered.

1.   The Angry Beast

"How dare you say that it isn't my fault!"

These manipulators never get blamed for anything. They use anger as their guard. Teenagers will often show these tendencies, but they aren't aware of this behavior and they typically grow out of it. Manipulators, on the other hand, deliberately show anger.

Oftentimes, in a romantic relationship, one partner will express anger if asked about credit card bills or cheating. No matter how nicely you bring up the topic, they will always respond over the top.

1.   Strong Dependents

"Please follow what I say in order to save me from my life."

These manipulators are both weak and strong. They make themselves appear like a powerless creature, but they are more in control than they appear. They want to depend on others to take care of them. In order to do this, they show their self as weak and unable to function on their own. Compliments are their secret weapon.

As soon as you see them as inferior and try to help them, they gain control. Slowly, all of their responsibilities become yours. If you try to avoid any of them, they cause you to feel like you are letting them down.

1.   The Perpetual Victim

"I get hurt and used by others all of the time."

In every aspect of their life, they will show themselves as a victim. Even if what happened had nothing to do with the manipulator, they will find some way to become the victim. If you were to accidentally cut yourself, the manipulator suddenly has a headache and it's your fault.

1.   The Expert

"I am better at everything than you."

They want to be on top of every situation. They are driven by their desire to attain social dominance over their victim. They have a strong ego and they blend it in with their ability to find vulnerable people. They lack to surround their self with people who have low self-confidence.

They use put-downs and insults to exploit the vulnerabilities of their victims. They hide their arrogance behind fake politeness. At their core, they have a lot of shame and self-doubt.

6

Chapter 6 How to Modify Your Behavior

"If there were a clear prospect that such evils were part of a barbarian past, then at least we might find a small crumb of comfort. No such prospect exists: no scientific analysis can even remotely answer or account for past and present horrors of human behaviour" - Simon Conway Morris

Body language is an important aspect of non-verbal communication, which is exactly the reason why people generally insist on in person meetings when they have to discuss something important. There is a need to note a person's expressions, gestures, posture, voice tone and more to know more about how they feel from within.

Here are some power-packed tips for influencing and manipulating people with the help of body language.

Keep your body language confident, self-assured and assertive. If your body language appears hesitant, inhibited, full of self-doubt and sloppy, there's little chance people are going to take you seriously. Always keep an upright posture. Keep your arms and legs uncrossed while talking to people. Your palms should stay open most of the time. Maintain a relaxed yet confident posture if you want people to trust you.

Always lean towards the other person while talking to show your interest in them. Tilt your head in their direction. Maintain a distance though, and don't thrust your face on theirs! Point your feet towards the subject's direction since it reveals interest and attention. Avoid invading a person's private space by getting too physically close to them too soon or they are less likely to trust you. Tilt your body slightly towards their direction or lean over a table to demonstrate your interest.

To create an instant rapport with a person, always align your body language with theirs. Face the person directly while speaking to reveal your interest and attention. This makes you come across as more affable, likeable and attentive, which in turn helps build a favorable rapport with the other person. This is even truer when you are communicating with a single person within a group setting. If you want to demonstrate interest in a person, face the person directly and align your body language with his or her body language. This will make them more receptive to what you say.

Always look a person right in the eye while speaking. Maintain eye contact throughout your communication with them. Shifting your gaze away from them frequently will make you come across as deceitful and dishonest. Similarly, from the person occasionally, but in general keep your gaze fixated on them while talking.

Stay attentive, interested and relaxed. Don't fidget with your fingers, tap your feet or play with objects. It gives the message that you are disconnected or disinterested in what the person is saying. These are also signs of nervousness. Let your hands and legs stay in a relaxed position.

When it comes to winning people, nothing works its charm as effectively as a smile. It is a wonderful ice-breaker and allows you to build a rapport with the other person on a subconscious level. Have a smile permanently fixed on your face while talking to people. It boosts your likeability factor.

A great tip for enhancing your body language when it comes to influencing, persuading and manipulating people is practice before a mirror. It lets you determine how you look while speaking to and interacting with other people. You can make the required changes to appear more influential and persuasive.

Observe closely your expressions, postures, tone, gestures, words and voice while speaking. Does it have the intended effect on a person? Does your confidence and conviction come across while talking to a person? Does your speech influence others into taking immediate action? Are people inspired by what you say?

Another powerful technique for observing your body language, expressions, gestures and voice is to record important presentations, negotiations and meetings. Closely examine your body language at these meetings. Do you come across as persuasive, convincing and forceful in your communication? Do you inspire other people's trust and conviction through your body language? This way you can make the necessary changes for altering your communication pattern to make it even more impactful.

Each time you are introduced to someone, demonstrate confidence and authority subconsciously through a firm handshake. Don't crush the person's hand or you'll come across as aggressive, and don't offer a limp handshake, which makes you appear unsure, low on confidence and inhibited. Stick to a handshake that is establishes your confidence and assertiveness.

Use power poses to your advantage. Social psychologist Amy Cuddy has spoken at length about how specific power poses help elevate our body's testosterone levels, and lower the stress inducing cortisol levels in as little as two minutes. These poses have a direct bearing on how we think and feel. Generally, these poses comprise forming broader body postures or occupying greater space or making your frame appear huge. By occupying greater physical space, you firmly establish yourself as a more authoritative and powerful person subconsciously.

Widen your stance slightly while standing so that your feet are apart. This makes you come across as a more powerful and confident personality. If you keep your feet firmly closely held together, you come across as insecure, nervous and anxious, which isn't very effective when it comes to influencing people.

Use your hands to enhance your speech. Brain research has pointed to the fact that the brain's broca region, which is significant for speech generation is stimulated when we use our hands or wave in an animated manner. Therefore, speech production and gestures are inextricably connected. Thus, we facilitate our words, thoughts, ideas and expressions through the use of hand gestures, making us even more effective communicators. Try to use your hands in animated gestures throughout the speech to improve the quality of your content significantly. You speech will possess better clarity and more impactful words/expressions.

Chapter 7 Difference Between Manipulation And Persuasion

"I'm not in love, but I'm open to persuasion" - Boy George

Manipulation and persuasion are closely related. In fact, the two words are sometimes used interchangeably in casual conversations. Even in psychological literature, the line between the two concepts can blur at times. To truly understand the difference between these two concepts, we have to look at their dictionary definitions.

The simplest definition for the term persuasion is "the act of causing a person or a group of people to do something or to believe something."

Based on that definition, you can see that persuasion is something that is done every day, and it's fair to say that it's often done out of self-interest. When you persuade someone to change what they believe about something, the outcome is clearly meant to benefit whoever initiates the act of persuasion.

In as much as it's borne out of self-interest, persuasion is has a certain purity about it; it is not at all evil, and it is completely socially acceptable. In fact, it's a core part of social discourse; for example, leaders have to persuade people to vote for them.

Persuasion is not at all immoral, and even though it's often done out of self-interest, it's possible for someone to do it with altruistic intentions; for example, civil rights leaders persuade people to join their causes, not because it benefits them, but because it benefits other people.

Manipulation, on the other hand, is defined as "to change something by artful or unfair means in order to serve one's purposes."

In this case, the underlying self-interest is unquestionable. Even if the manipulative action you take is for someone else's own good, the bottom line is that it benefits you as well. The benefit that a third party or the target of the manipulation may gain in that case is a mere byproduct of, and the main goal is to benefit the manipulator.

Where manipulation is involved, there is a clear implication that the manipulator wants what he wants, no matter the consequences. That is why, unlike persuasion, manipulation makes use of techniques that are deceptive; the target is deliberately misinformed to increase his or her chances of making certain choices.

In general, psychologists agree that the difference between manipulation and persuasion comes down to 3 key things. The first thing is the intent of the person who instigates the persuasive or manipulative action. The second thing is transparency or the truthfulness that goes into the persuasion or manipulation process. The third thing is the net-benefit that results from the persuasive or manipulative action. In persuasion, the intent is generally constructive, while in manipulation, the intent is generally destructive. In persuasion, there is a lot of transparency and truthfulness, while in manipulation; there is a lot of deception and half-truths. In persuasion, the resultant action benefits all parties, but in manipulation, the resultant action benefits the manipulator a lot more than the target.

If someone describes you as manipulative, you will take it as a criticism. However, if he described you as persuasive, you will take it as a compliment. When you tell someone that you have been manipulated, in their mind, they'll register that information as a complaint. However, if you tell someone that you have been persuaded, they will think that you have arrived at a certain conclusion after objectively reviewing the evidence as it was presented to you.

Manipulation is thought to be immoral because it harms the person on the receiving end of the manipulative action. Sometimes manipulation can hide under the guise of persuasion, and that is when it is most harmful. Take the example of advertising. We tend to think of advertising as persuasion, or a fairly harmless form of social influence. However, when the company that creates the product hides crucial information from the customer, or if they lie about the benefits of their product in their advert, then that is manipulation.

For example, when big tobacco companies hid the harmful effects of tobacco from the public, or when they pushed back against scientific research in order to maintain the popularity of their products, that was manipulation, and not persuasion.

When advertising is based on truth and in scientific evidence, then that is persuasion. However, when it encourages people to form beliefs that are objectively untrue, that is manipulation.

Even when manipulation is used to help others, it still seems morally objectionable. For example, if you notice that your friend is in a toxic relationship, and then you manipulate her into breaking up with her partner, even if she is better for it, you will still feel like you have done something wrong. That brings us to an important difference between manipulation and persuasion; how the two concepts relate to free will.

In the example about, you may help your friend by manipulating her into breaking up with her toxic boyfriend, but in doing so;

you have subverted her free will. When you manipulate someone, you technically make a choice for them, and they end up thinking that they made a choice by themselves. However, when you persuade someone, you present them with all the information they need to make the right choice. So, if you manipulate your friend into ending her relationship, even if the outcome benefits her, morally speaking, you end up having a lot in common with the toxic boyfriend you are trying to save her from. You are like a police officer who is willing to break the law in order to catch lawbreakers.

Now that you understand the difference between manipulation and persuasion, and you know the shortcomings of manipulation as an influence technique, should you continue using both manipulation and persuasion? Well, when it comes to persuasion, there is no objective reason why you should stop using it. However, where manipulation is concerned, you need to have an introspective debate with yourself and try to judge each situation on a case by case basis. Supposing you are a salesman and your livelihood depends on manipulation, will you stop using it? What if you are in a competitive workplace and the trajectory of your career depends on your ability to manipulate people; are you going to limit yourself to persuasion? Ultimately, it's up to you to decide what you can live with.

Chapter 8 Mind Control

"To enjoy good health, to bring true happiness to one's family, to bring peace to all, one must first discipline and control one's own mind. If a man can control his mind he can find the way to Enlightenment, and all wisdom and virtue will naturally come to him" - Buddha

The term mind control has many definitions and interpretations, but the crucial thing to note is that it doesn't involve any sort of magic or supernatural ability; it just requires a rudimentary understanding of human emotions and behavior. Mind control can involve brainwashing a person, reeducating them, reforming their thoughts, using coercive techniques to persuade them of certain things, or brain-sweeping. There are many forms of mind control, and we could fill an entire book discussing all those forms, but for our purposes, we will look at the concept in general terms. Mind control means a person is trying to get others to feel, think, or behave in a certain way, or to react and make decisions following a certain pattern. It could vary from a girl trying to get her boyfriend to develop certain habits, to a cult leader trying to convince his followers that he is God.

Mind control is based on one thing: information. We have the thoughts and beliefs that we do because we learned them. When we are subjected to new information on a deliberate and consistent basis, it's possible to alter our beliefs, thoughts, or even memories. The brain is hardwired to survive, and towards that end, it's very good at learning information that is crucial for our survival. When you receive certain information consistently, your brain will start to believe it even if you know it's not true. For example, even if you are the most rational person out there, if you go online and watch 100 videos about a certain conspiracy theory, you will start to believe it to some extent. That explains why people who seem smart can end up getting indoctrinated into cults or even terrorist groups.

Mind control also works more effectively when one is dependent on the person who is trying to control his/her mind. Even in relationships that are involuntary, the victim can start buying the perpetrator's world view if they have been dependent on the perpetrator for a long time. That explains phenomena such as Stockholm syndrome (where people who are kidnapped or held hostage start being affectionate towards their captors and empathizing with their causes). The worst thing you can do is assume that you are too smart for mind control to work on you. Under the right circumstances, anyone can be persuaded to abandon their world view and adopt someone else's. Mind games are covert tricks that are deliberately crafted in order to manipulate someone. Think of them as "handcrafted" psychological manipulation techniques. While other techniques are applied broadly, mind games are created to target very specific people. They work best when the victim trusts the perpetrator, and the perpetrator understands the victim's personality and behavior. Most of the psychological manipulation techniques we have discussed thus far can be used when crafting mind games. A person who understands you will tell you certain things or behave in certain ways around you because they are deliberately trying to get you to react in a certain way. It almost always involves feigning certain emotions.

People who play mind games use innocent sounding communication to elicit calculated reactions from you. Psychologists refer to such mind games as "conscious one-upmanship," and they have observed that they occur in all areas of life. Mind games occur in office politics, personal relationships, and even in international diplomacy. At work, someone could try to make you feel like you are not up to the task so that they can steal an opportunity from you. In a marriage, your partner could make certain seemingly innocent slights against you so that you feel like you have something to prove, and you take a certain course of action as a result. In dating, there are "pickup artists" who use different kinds of tricks to get you to lower your guard and let them in. Mind control is not the whole of the vague information you hear in gossip, accompanied by conspiracy theories. It is the product of secret experiments with systematic studies dating back to World War II, perhaps older. Of course, the 20th-century totalitarian regimes, who wanted to robotize their subjects, also played a major role in this. Therefore, the first thing to note is that developing technology facilitates the mind-control efforts of the oppressors every year. Like Telegram scourge that happens today... But mind control; it is something that can be done without technology with the support of psychology and orator. The most striking example of this in history; this is the work carried out by Goebbels, the Minister of Propaganda of the Nazis. Goebbels succeeded in engraving his name in gold letters in this lane, which was the disgrace of humanity.

Mind control; It is the name given to all the unethical activities of some power centers to manage people in line with their goals, to shape their ideas and control their lifestyles. While technological opportunities can be utilized in mind control, human psychology, propaganda knowledge, and social engineering are essential. Also, mind control; it is applied in a highly systematic, insidious way by people who have done as much research as required by a master or doctor. In other words, it is essential that people don't realize the engineering applied to them, so to be hypnotized. Therefore, it is challenging to recognize and resist. Also; every political and intellectual propaganda is not minded control. Mind control, as we mentioned above, is a different matter.

Effects of Mind Control on human

The effects of using mind control on human beings are seen in different ways. Some of them are as follows;

• "Memory loss and behavior disorders

• Change in direction, intensity and content of sound heard

• Speech deterioration by checking eyelids

• Severe heart palpitations

• Forcing accidents on the shoulders and arms during laborious work

• Jogging of the elbows and preventing work while doing something

• Pain and unnecessary movement of the legs, right and left swing and excessive stiffness

• Itching and blushing in hard-to-reach areas

• Contractions of large muscles in the back

• Checking hand gestures

• Reading thoughts or transmitting thoughts from outside

• Seeing moving imaginary images

• Keeping eyelids constantly open

• Continuous tinnitus

• Jaw and teeth shivering for no reason

Chapter 9 Victims Of Manipulation

"When quick results are imperative, the manipulation of the masses through symbols may be the only quick way of having a critical thing done" - John Grierson

Just as predators have several traits they often all have, so to do their targets. The people that predators choose to target are typically chosen methodically, seeking out those who are least likely to rebel or try to fight back from any sort of manipulation. They can identify potential targets at a glance, needing little more than seconds to pass judgment on whether that person should be pursued with shocking accuracy. They can tell based off of body language, clothing, situations, interactions, and more, who will be able to serve them best, and they frequently act upon it. Here are some of the most common traits people who find themselves victims of manipulators often have.

Lacking Confidence

Due to lacking confidence, an individual can be quite easy to steamroll. Looking for body language that marks someone as lacking confident is a surefire way for predators to identify an easy target. Those who lack confidence are not likely to put up any sort of fight, either if you attack physically or emotionally. In lacking confidence, the predator can be sure that the individual also lacks the ability to defend boundaries or him or herself. When someone comes across as self-confident, he or she exudes an air of someone not as willing to put up with any sort of manipulation without a fight. Those with confidence will fight back when they feel wronged, violated, or hurt, and would have no qualms walking away from a relationship because they trust their own judgment.

By seeking someone lacking confidence, a predator goes after the easiest possible target to get whatever is desired, whether it is physical affection, arm candy, money, a home, a sale, a vote, or even just the feeling of having dominated someone else. The predator is able to boost his or her own ego through completely taking over another person's life and making decisions for the person. They may want someone around that will always defer to them, allowing them a position of power, even if it is undeserved or unwarranted. They may want someone to make them feel better about themselves, and someone with low self-confidence is likely to do that.

Sometimes, however, predators will go out of their way to identify someone with higher levels of confidence, as they see it as a game. They make it a challenge to so thoroughly break someone with high confidence that the target allows them to dominate the situation. This predator is doing nothing more than toying with the target and seeks nothing but self-gratification from doing so.

Have Something Desirable

Sometimes, personality has nothing to do with being targets. Sometimes, predators go after someone because they have something the predator wants. Whether it is money, status, a relationship, or anything else, the predator may choose to go after that person in hopes of getting it by association. If the person is someone powerful or influential, the predator may weasel her way into a friendship with the sole intention of pulling from that person's influence in the future. By winning what the other person perceives as a friendship, the manipulator creates an arsenal of people with a wide range of skills, abilities, and prestige that can be used when the need arises. If she wants a new job, she may be able to get a friend to pull strings and get her one, for example.

If what she desires is money, she may worm her way into a friendship or relationship with someone that has a lot of money in an attempt to attract that kind of lifestyle. If her boyfriend is wealthy, he would likely have little issue spending money on her. Further, she may feel as though associating herself with people who have what she wants will help her learn how to achieve what the other people have. Through learning what people are doing and how they are doing it, she may be able to emulate those behaviors in hopes of getting what she wants.

Caregiver-type

Some people are more prone to being caregivers than others. People who are compassionate can become easily manipulated because they seek to believe the best in others and seek to ensure that others' needs are met as thoroughly as possible. The caregiver-type person is likely to see the manipulator and all of his or her flaws, but proceed with a relationship anyway; believing that all that is needed to remedy the situation is love and patience. Unfortunately, that resilience to make sure that the manipulator is cared for and nurtured back to mental health also makes the caregiver an easy victim as well.

Because the caregiver is willing to take all of that negative behavior as signs that the manipulator needs more help, he or she will often completely overlook the warning signs and endure the manipulation, feeling as though it will stop eventually. Unfortunately, no amount of love or patience is going to change who someone is, and they are likely to be disappointed as the manipulative behaviors continue to grow, eventually beginning to drain on even the caregiver, whose personality type is prone to patience and resilience.

This is yet another common target for the manipulator because he or she can get away with far worse behavior far quicker than imagined. Because the manipulator knows that very little done will actually successfully push the caregiver away due to the caregiver's own inherent desire to fix the manipulator, the parasitic manipulator is able to continue to draw upon the caregiver's goodwill to get anything desired with few repercussions.

Empathetic

Considering that most of the manipulators you will encounter either lack empathy or know how to turn off their empathy to steel themselves from other people's emotional states, it should come as no surprise that they are naturally drawn toward the empathetic.

Empathy is the ability to sense and really understand how someone else is feeling. It is as if you have taken yourself and placed yourself in the other person's shoes, understanding exactly how they feel because you know how you would feel in their situation. This sense of putting yourself in someone else's shoes enables humans to ensure that those within their family or tribal unit are taken care of. It extends to other people as well, and those who are particularly empathetic find themselves identifying with other people. They may see the manipulator and decide that they see a person who is clearly in dire need of love and attention. They see the manipulator's flaws and want to try to fix them because they understand how lonely or down they would feel if they lacked confidence, lacked friends and family, or lacked whatever else it is that they believe the manipulator may be lacking.

The empathetic individual, like the caregiver, will take more than his or her fair share of abuse, justifying it as the manipulator being in a bad situation and that any rational person who had suffered the same way would behave similarly. The empathetic target is also far more susceptible to mind games relating to emotions and guilt trips, and the empathetic nature of the individual is eventually used as a weapon against him- or herself.

Dysfunctional Upbringing

People who have grown up in dysfunction have the disadvantage of never learning what normal, functioning, healthy relationships entail. They typically associate their own upbringing with what is normal and seek to replicate those sorts of relationships in adulthood. If a child grew up around parents who fought and argued all the time, with the mother always giving up what she wanted while the father took endlessly, the newfound adult is going to attempt to replicate that dynamic in any adult relationships.

Likewise, someone who grew up in dysfunction is not likely to understand how to set normal or healthy boundaries, or how to enforce those boundaries. They will be easily steamrolled, especially if boundaries being disrespected were a common theme growing up. This leaves the individual quite vulnerable, as he has no sense of normalcy and no sense of how to protect himself within a relationship. He does not understand that relationships are supposed to be symbiotic, and because of that, he is far more likely to deal with misbehaviors and abuse from a manipulator.

Knowing this, manipulators look for those who grew up in dysfunction. They are seen as easy targets. Their lack of boundaries make them easier to manipulate, and their lack of confidence or sense of what a healthy relationship looks like means that the target is not likely to see red flags when the manipulative behaviors begin cropping up. With red flags unseen, the manipulation is not seen as a warning sign that the relationship is unhealthy or should be ended. Particularly if abuse and manipulation were prevalent in childhood, the target may actually have a high tolerance for such behaviors, meaning the predator can escalate quickly and more effectively.

How to identify yourself as the Victim of Covert Manipulation

No one likes being manipulated. When manipulation occurs, you lose your power and your will. You must do what the other person wants. You often have no idea what the other person is really planning and you have no say in the situation. This makes life very difficult and it can cause you to do things that you don't want to do.

Now that you know the secrets to covert manipulation, you also know what to watch out for. You can reverse the techniques in this book to see when others are manipulating you. You can also flip these tactics on people and give them the manipulation that they are trying to run on you. There are various ways that you can protect yourself against manipulators.

Identify when You are a Victim

Everyone has a gut instinct that rears up when they are being used or misguided. Your gut instinct is very sound. You will know when you are a victim. The problem is, a lot of people ignore their instincts. You might ignore yours. You might think something like, "I'm just being paranoid" or "What could possibly go wrong if I hang out with this person?" You might think that the harm will be worth the benefits that you could get from knowing this person who gives you bad vibes. Maybe everyone else likes this guy, so you think that you are just being weird and you should like him too. Or maybe he is able to charm you and convince you that he is not so bad and over time you start to get over your initial bad vibes.

But vibes are not something that you should ever ignore. The minute your gut warns you about someone, listen. Your first impression of someone is never wrong. If you get a bad first impression, don't give the person a second chance. You know more about someone by just glancing at them than you would think. The human brain is amazingly powerful; you only are conscious of roughly ten percent of your brain, so there is a lot going on under the surface that you are not consciously aware of.

Your brain is capable of reading people and determining the future far more than you realize.

So when you get that gut feeling, understand that your brain is working very hard and noticing things that you are not consciously aware of. The person that you get bad vibes may not be matching his body language to his words, or he may be acting oddly in ways that you can't detect easily. Listen to your gut!

If you are just not in touch with your gut at all, or if you have doubts about someone, you might want to consider looking at some other signs. You can identify a manipulator based on his actions and language choices. You can also tell by how you feel around this person. There are various clues that point out who someone really is and what his intentions are.

What Makes You Vulnerable

You may wonder why manipulators are attracted to you, especially if you have had multiple encounters with manipulative types. You may also wonder what you should change about yourself to avoid running into a manipulator in the future.

One thing that makes you vulnerable is being accepting of manipulative treatment and emotional abuse. If you were emotionally abused or repressed as a child, this type of treatment may seem normal to you. You don't know anything else. You don't how a healthy relationship is supposed to feel. So you accept the terrible treatment that others would not think of accepting. As a result, you are projecting a sense of vulnerability that draws manipulators from far away. The minute you begin to tolerate their treatment and keep them in your life, they gain power over you and choose to keep using you until they get what they want. Work on increasing your self-esteem and avoiding familiar patterns. If you get that eerie sense of déjà vu when you meet someone, you might want to avoid that person because he is probably reminding you of previous abusive patterns that you have been in.

Another thing that may make you vulnerable is neediness or weakness. If you are in a vulnerable time in life, you might be more open to manipulators. Manipulators can see that you are in need and they see it as an opportunity to offer you what you need in exchange of what they really want. They will use any opportunity to gain control over you, and when you are in a bad period of life, you basically hand them opportunities. You need to guard your heart and mind especially well when you are at a disadvantage. Be wary of extremely kind strangers or life savers. Not all heroes are good guys. Your heroes may help you, but they may have hidden intentions. Most people won't do something for free so watch out.

You may also be a target for manipulation if you have low self-esteem. Events in your life or your childhood may have stripped away your self-esteem and confidence. You may be emotionally vulnerable. So you want people who build up your ego. Manipulators can spot this and they will move in on you, working hard to please you and make you smile. They see a way into your mind through your bruised ego. Try to build your self-esteem by yourself and work on loving yourself.

Signs of a Manipulator

A manipulator is often incredibly superficial. This means that he looks good on the outside, but there is nothing to follow it up on the inside. He is shallow and lacks depth. Everything he does and says is fake, part of a façade that he erects to fool you. So beware of people who are incredibly charming and attractive when you first meet them. Get to know them before you start confiding in them or trusting them. Don't make a commitment or business deal until you are absolutely sure of yourself.

Another sign of a manipulator is that you feel compelled to confide in him or to do what he wants. You constantly find yourself saying yes when you want to say no. It's impossible to be yourself and to stand up for yourself. He has some sort of power over you that you can't resist. Unfortunately, this power is just a carefully woven web of manipulation, deception, and emotional harm. He will dump you the minute he gets all that he can from you, so don't stick around or make the mistake of thinking that this relationship will last. He does not care, no matter how well he pretends to. Get away from him before the relationship gets too harmful and he ruins your life.

You may also find yourself saying sorry all of the time. Your guilt eats you up. Every situation with this person seems like your fault. Even if he is at fault, he manages to twist things around so that you feel guilty. He will never take responsibility for anything that he does and he will always put everything on you. He can do what he wants, but he holds you to exacting standards and punishes you when you don't follow suit. He basically kills your self-esteem and causes you to hate yourself.

Finally, a manipulator is great at changing your mind. You might feel one way, but after talking with him, you feel a completely different way. He is able to change your mind and your way of thinking. Sometimes this may even be a good thing, as he makes you think more constructively or positively. But be wary of someone who has so much power over your moods and your thoughts.

What Manipulation Feels Like

Often, in the early stages of a manipulative or emotionally abusive relationship, you will feel amazing. Your manipulator will be an expert at making you feel good about yourself. He will flatter you and fuel your ego.

Some people out there will make you feel good because they genuinely love you. But it often takes times for such a relationship to build. If someone whom you barely know is suddenly super into you and trying to rush a relationship, become very wary. Don't let things move too quickly. Get to know the person first. Someone who wants you so badly right off of the bat is usually superficial and just trying to prime you into a victim. Don't fall for it. Normal people don't just jump into relationships or try to rush things. Normal people also don't start acting crazy about you in an unusually short period of time.

A manipulator will make you feel like there are butterflies in your stomach. You will strive to please him. Your biggest desire will be to make him smile. This is because he is already making you feel as if you owe him or as if you like him so much that you will work to please him. Beware of people who make you feel like a puppet. You should never want to bend over backwards for someone so urgently. You need to have a sense of dignity and personal space and value in every relationship. If you don't, something is off.

You will also feel guilty about the smallest things. You may feel inadequate or guilty for not always pleasing this person every day. A sense of guilt about living or being you may haunt you. You may feel ashamed of who you are. These feelings may seem to come out of the blue, but this is just because you are with a super covert manipulator. Trust me, he is playing some serious games with your heart to inspire your guilt. These feelings are not random or spontaneous, but rather part of your manipulator's carefully crafted plan to hurt you. So you should become suspicious and understand that these feelings are not a normal element of a healthy relationship.

Your self-esteem will certainly dive when you spend time around a manipulator. Soon, your confidence will become riddled with holes. You will be poisoned with self-doubt and angst. This is not a good thing and you should not stay around someone who does this to you.

You also will probably start to feel crazy. You will wonder if you have an undiagnosed disorder or if you are falling apart at the seams. When you argue with this person, he will deny everything that he just said. He will call you nuts for arguing with him or claim that you are just making things up. In addition, he will invent elaborate stories and blame you for things that you never did, often so convincingly that you start to believe that you did what he claims. He will also challenge your perception of reality, lie through his teeth, and make you question yourself constantly. All of these things combined will tear at your self-esteem and consciousness, making you question your sanity. Manipulators can actually rewire the neurons of your brain and do permanent damage to your mental health and personality, so you should not stick around.

One great piece of advice is that if you feel the need to record someone during arguments because he denies what he says later and makes you feel crazy, then you are in an emotionally abusive relationship and you should leave now. You are not crazy. This person is just gaslighting you.

What to Do when Someone is Manipulating You

The simplest piece of advice on how to deal with a manipulator is to just up and leave. If you can do this, great. You should immediately. There will be no good to come from this relationship, so why stay around and get hurt?

But this advice is often easier said than done. There are some situations where you cannot escape a manipulator and his traps. For instance, you might have to work with a manipulator and you can't just quit your job, or you don't want to. Or you might have a manipulative family member and you can't cut him off or you will lose all of your family. You may feel trapped and unable to leave for various reasons, such as financial reasons. Maybe you have kids with the manipulator and must speak to him or her for the rest of your life regarding the children. Co-parenting doesn't automatically end when your children turn eighteen; sometimes, you have to continue a relationship with the father or mother well into your children's' adult lives, and you must be around each other for your children's weddings, graduations, grandchildren, etc. Or maybe there is a manipulative friend in your group whom everyone else likes. There are countless reasons why you may be stuck with a manipulator in your life. Leaving is not always a viable option.

Having a Manipulative Partner and How to Avoid Manipulation

What is a Narcissistic Personality?

The word 'narcissist' comes from a story in Greek mythology, where Narcissus fell in love with his own image. The narcissistic personality is defined as a person who idealized their own self-image and attributes to the point of negatively affecting other people's lives. Many people possess narcissistic traits when it has to do with a certain section of their lives, but also possess a healthy dose of humility and self-doubt. This is not the case for a person with a narcissistic personality.

In 2004, psychiatrists Hotchkiss and James F. Masterson listed what they called the Seven Deadly Sins of Narcissism:

Lack of /bad boundaries: Boundaries simply do not exist for a person who is a full-blown narcissist. They are unaware that other people can exist not solely to suit their needs, and that other people may have different thoughts or feelings than themselves. Narcissistic supply is a term used to describe how narcissist relies on codependents in order to fill their sense of self-worth.

Exploitation: The narcissist may employ exploitation without regard for the feelings of others. This is usually done to another person who is in a position of subservience and cannot escape it, such as in a work setting or children at school.

Entitlement: Believing that they are special and deserve special treatment and begin expressing narcissistic rage they are denied it (a reaction when a threat to their self-worth is perceived).

Arrogance: A narcissist likes to raise their own self-importance by degrading others.

Envy: A narcissist may employ the feeling of contempt toward another person in order to avoid feelings of jealousy in reaction to the result of another person's achievements.

Magical Thinking: A psychological defense mechanism that allows them to see themselves as flawless and project shame onto others rather than feel it themselves.

Shamelessness: Narcissists do not express feeling shame for any behavior or belief they may possess, as the sensation of feeling shame implies that they must have done something wrong.

Narcissistic Personality Disorder (NPD)

NPD is a personality disorder that expresses a long-term pattern of behavior that is self-focused, superior, and exploitative of others and severely lacks empathy for others. The difference between NPD and the previously described traits of a person with a narcissistic personality is the consistency of the traits and to what extent they impair their lives. This difference is described as pathological; when the expression of these traits consistently disrupts the lives of the narcissist, it is when a mental health diagnosis is given. Many people possess narcissistic personality traits and are able to live a successful and stress-free life, while those with NPD may perceive themselves this way, are actually not developing and achieving success due to the crippling fear of criticism, self-doubt, and failure that lies under their inflated sense of self-worth.

The Malignant Narcissist

These kinds of narcissists are ones that are not bothered by guilt and has the ability to resemble antisocial personality disorder. APD is another personality disorder defined primarily by antisocial behavior that has no consideration for right and wrong. The malignant narcissist may take pleasure in causing pain and display forms of sadistic behavior. The key difference though between a malignant narcissist and an antisocial personality is the way the person relates to others. Narcissists share a codependent relationship with others, and deep down, require the approval of others in order to function. A person with antisocial personality disorder could not care less about the opinion of others and do not require the engagement of other people in order to feel validated.

The Narcissist and Emotional/Psychological Abuse: What Truly Lies Beneath

Abuse is the behavioral act that a narcissist applies as a defense mechanism against a variety of emotions that the narcissist is constantly attempting to suppress. Despite the outward expression of self-importance, grandiosity, lacking empathy, and cruel behavior, the narcissist is actually acting out of deeply repressed sensations of fear. They fear rejection, their own imperfections and shortcomings, of being abandoned, unwanted, and unloved.

The following section will summarize 14 behavioral expressions of a narcissist and how it connects to being abusive. A narcissist could be an authority figure, a parent, a partner, a teacher, a coach, or a caregiver. Marjalis Fjelstad writes about the behaviors to look out for if you believe someone in your life is a narcissist on Mind Body Green.

Narcissists feel the need to be the best/most at everything in their lives. Even if it means the sickest or injured, they must be at the top.

A narcissist constantly feels the need to acquire validation from a partner or important person in their lives because they subconsciously believed that they are not good enough. External validation is always required, but never enough. They will always want you to praise them because they cannot provide the confidence and assurance for themselves, despite the outward appearance of confidence and egotism.

Narcissists are perfectionists, which means that those in their lives must be perfect, they must be perfect, and everything that they have planned or envisioned for themselves must play out without a hitch. This, of course, is not how life works, which often leads to the narcissist feeling dissatisfied. Perfectionism is why it is endlessly difficult for a narcissist to receive any criticism, even if it is constructive.

Because of the perfectionism, narcissist wants to control everything around them, and this includes a partner, a child, a parent, etc. This is where control in abusive relationships comes from; because the behavior of the victim is not lining up with the exact ways the abuser wants it to.

Narcissists never take responsibility for their actions. Even if they contributed to the not so flawless way something may have been carried about, the fault is never their own. It is yours because you did do exactly as you were instructed. Nothing they ever do can be wrong.

As previously stated, a narcissist cannot comprehend what boundaries are. They cannot comprehend that you have your own thoughts, feelings, expectations, and past. They do not like when another person expresses feelings that oppose their own, because it is not perfect, which leads to more behaviors that attempt to control their entire world.

The narcissist lacks empathy, which is why they are unable to understand boundaries. They cannot correctly read body language or facial expressions because they believe that other people must feel the same way they do. However, they are also overly sensitive and aware of perceived rejection from others, and constantly believe that the source of their negative feelings is caused by the person they are closest to in their life.

Logic does not work with the narcissist. Trying to explain to a narcissist how their behavior affects you is futile because they are only aware of their own thoughts and feelings.

Splitting is a term used to describe how narcissists categorize every feeling, person, and experience into one of two categories: the good and the bad. This is due to their intense sense of perfectionism. Nothing can be a combination of a positive valence experience and a negatively perceived one. They can only cope with the single experience that is their own.

An appearance of surety and self-confidence hide the true narcissist experience of fear; fear of failure, losing money, their partner leaving them, their children being taken away, etc. No matter how close a person can get to a narcissist, they will never be able to build a trusting relationship, simply because the narcissist is in constant fear of being abandoned.

Anxiety is a looming sensation for the narcissist, who projects this sensation onto their siblings, partner, or parent. This is not an enjoyable sensation for the narcissist, so they rather throw it onto someone else.

Shamelessness may appear to be a trait of the narcissist, but it is truly an expression of the opposite. Shame means that there is something wrong about a person, and the narcissist cannot cope with this notion. Feeling shame is the enemy, so they do not allow themselves to feel it and bury it deep inside their subconscious. They hate that they possess insecurities and fear, and live with this lingering sensation that becomes projected on the closest loved one who may 'find them out.'

Since the narcissist doesn't want to accept that they feel fear or insecurities, they are unable to feel vulnerable. This makes it difficult to create and maintain close intimate relationships. The narcissist is constantly displaying this flawless sense of self-importance and perfection to the point where the true human beneath that is hidden from those that the narcissist considers the most important.

Lack of empathy means that the narcissist cannot work or communicate in a group setting, because only their wants, needs, and thoughts are what truly exists in their world.

Chapter 10   Common Traits of A Manipulator

"I learned more complex ways to manipulate the manipulators, to bring attention to issues about which I felt passionate" - Joey Skaggs

Most master manipulators have mastered the art of deception. In many cases, these people will appear sincere and respectable but that is just a façade they use to get their way. They will use tricks to attract, trap and ensnare you in a manipulative relationship before you see their true colors. Truth be told, the manipulative person is not interested in you or your life, rather you are just a vehicle to carry out the work of the manipulator. You become a part of their plans without your own consent or understanding.

Manipulators have several ways of getting to the victim and you might not identify them easily. Basically, they take what you say and do and turn it around to something you cannot even relate to. They will then hold it on your head. A large number of manipulators will attempt to make you feel confused and even crazy. The manipulators distort the truth and will resort to ruthless lying if it will help them meet their goals.

A manipulative person will play the victim and make you appear like the cause of the problem. In fact, you will find yourself apologizing to the manipulator while he/she is actually causing the problem. A manipulator will hardly ever take responsibility for his/her actions. He/she will be nice in one minute, passive-aggressive in the other and standoffish in the next. This technique will keep you guessing and feeling confused about your stand. The manipulator will make you feel insecure and defensive.

In other cases, the manipulator will become vicious and aggressive, resorting to criticism, and personal attacks to make you do what they want. A good number of them also use threats and bullying and if you do not resist their techniques, they drain your energy. Below are some of the common traits of manipulators. By understanding them, you will know what to watch out for when you suspect that a person is manipulating you. Understanding these basic mechanisms of the manipulator will help you stay out of manipulative relationships. Being alert and staying true to what you know and believe can help you deal with the manipulator. The list below will help you anticipate the behavior of manipulators and maintain n your own integrity in their presence.

First, manipulators either believe that their way of doing things is the best or, they just lack insight on how to deal with other people. The most important thing to a manipulator is getting things done in his/her way regardless of the scenario. It does not matter who gets hurt so long as the manipulator wins. Ultimately, every relationship, situation, and conversation is about them. It does not matter what the other person thinks, wants or does. According to Darlene Ouimet, a controller, abuser, and a manipulative person do not question him/herself. These categories of people do not ever think they are the problem in any situation. They will always point someone else as the cause of the mistake.

Secondly, Manipulative people do not care about boundaries. To them, other people do not have feelings and they are just available. The manipulator is relentless in his/her pursuit of goals and does not care who gets hurt along the way. As such, the manipulator will crowd your space, emotionally, physically, psychologically and spiritually and not feel concerned or remorseful. Most of the manipulators lack the understanding of personal space and respect for identity. Some understand these concepts but do not care. Manipulators can be likened to parasites – acceptable in nature but not in the world of human behavior. Feeding off someone without their consent will drain, exhaust, deplete, demean and weaken the victim.

Thirdly, a manipulator does not take responsibility for his/her own conduct and will always blame others for his/her faults. It is not that the manipulative person does not understand responsibility; rather, he/she avoids it. In fact, he/she will make you accept all your faults and even pay for them but will never admit to his/hers. Ultimately, they will use your faults to make you do fulfill their needs at the expense of yours. They leave you no room for meeting your own goals.

Fourthly, manipulative people prey on the emotional sensitivity, sensibility, and conscientiousness of others. They understand that you will most likely want to help because you are kind and caring. Consequently, they will hook you into a relationship and because of your good human nature; you will want to help a 'friend'. At first, the manipulator will make you feel like a hero, appreciated, and praised due to your efforts. He/she will make you feel like a very good person because you are kind and helpful. However, these compliments will reduce with time because the manipulator does not care about you, only what you are doing

Fifth, manipulative people have a way of communication which will alert you. Pay attention to how a person talks about others in relation to you. The way a person talks to you about others is the same way he/she talks about you in front of others. A manipulator is good at triangulation and will easily create situations and scenarios allowing for rivalry, intrigue, and jealousy. Unlike empathetic people, manipulators promote and encourage disharmony.

Sixth, manipulators will always act as if they cannot understand you. If you turn them down, they will demand an explanation. Do not waste your time explaining yourself to other people especially if they are committed to misunderstanding and manipulating your words and actions. Do not wait for a person to understand and like you – a manipulator is just not interested in what you are, only what you can do.

Note that;

If you characterize people by their actions rather than words, it will be easier to identify a manipulator. Most manipulators will not keep their word. By understanding that manipulators make promises they have no intention of keeping, you will easily identify and walk away from their traps. Observe people closely and do not make excuses for their character – Usually, what you see is what you get.

If someone can put in so much effort in pretense, then he/she is capable of being a good person. However, it is not up to you to change a manipulative person. You may drop hints to them about their inappropriate behavior, but do not engage in full combat mode – Engaging them more will leave room for more manipulation.

Essentially, our first encounter and perception of a person strongly paint how we develop a relationship with them. If we are to understand from the beginning that the individual in question is only putting on a façade to get to us, - and to appear socially acceptable. We would know when to say no. Knowing when a person is faking it will help us to stay wary of how much we get involved in the self-centered skims.

Finally, it is important for us to keep examining what we believe. You will realize that your beliefs change with time. As we grow up, the illusion of father charismas and Easter bunny becomes less vivid. It is important for everyone to assess the ways life changes are affecting his/her ideas. When you are unsure of what you believe, it is easy to be swayed by a manipulator. However, if you acknowledge that life is changing in a particular way, it will be easier to deal with ambushes from manipulators.

Chapter 11   How to Manipulate People

"Tactics are manipulative" - Shiv Khera

There are going to be certain times in your life when you will find that manipulation is going to come in handy. While you know that it is so important to practice in as many scenarios as you can, there are going to be ones that you will find manipulation will be the most useful. In this chapter, we are going to focus on the best places where you can use the skills of manipulation so that you can get ahead and really benefit from the things that you have learned so far.

Business Negotiations

When it comes to working on some negotiations in business, it is easy to see how you want to make sure that you can get your way. Getting your own way will usually mean that you want to close a better deal, one that is going to be highly favorable to your own company. Closing these deals, and making sure that they are in your favor, will mean that your company is able to get most, if not all, of the things that it is asking for, and that you will barely have to deal with any inconveniences in the process to do this.

There are a lot of things that you can negotiate during these meetings, such as better terms on the deals, better pricing on the services, and more, and if you use your skills in manipulation, you are more likely to get the whole thing to work in your favor.

When it comes to negotiating on some better deals for the business, you will find that manipulation is a very powerful tool for you to use. Whether others like to admit to this or not, negotiations are rarely fair, and there is usually going to be a person who comes out on top. You want to make sure that the person who comes out on top is you.

When you use manipulation in these efforts, it means that you are easily able to dominate the conversation, without the other person even realizing it. When this happens, others in the negotiation are more likely to give in without even doing a fight, because they think they are getting something good out of it as well. Because of this, and all of the good benefits that you can get from this, you should bring out the manipulation skills that you learn as much as possible when you are working with a business negotiation.

Closing Sales

If you are at all involved in a sales process at some point, then you know that it is not always easy to close sales. If you work in retail, for example, you likely notice that many of the people who come into your store are dreaming and looking around, and sometimes, they won't be prepared to buy anything. Because of this, it can sometimes be valuable to know how to manipulate people as you can encourage them to spend money that they did not otherwise intend to spend.

What this means is that when you get the other person to purchase something through your manipulation techniques, it results in more sales for the business. If you are the one who owns the company, you know how important this is. If you are an employee, you know that effective numbers of sales, and good sales strategies, means that you are more likely to be respected by your employer, and then you can make it up the ladder of the company.

If you are in a sales position that is considered business to business, then you know that manipulation is so important. People who end up going to a meeting with you are likely interested in what you are going to offer, but they could also be shopping around to a few different companies at the same time, and you need to find ways that will put your business ahead of all the other choices that they are considering.

Knowing how to use the right skills of manipulation at any level of sales means that they can close more deals and that they will be left with happier customers. This only means that good things are going to be available for you in the future.

Getting Prices That Are Better

You can use manipulation from the other side of the perspective as well. If you are the customer and knowing how to manipulate during this time can be highly valuable. As you know, many times the salespeople have been given some room to negotiate with their customers in order to encourage sales. This means that if you are willing to use some manipulation and work with them, you can get a special and better deal. You are able just to take the price, but wouldn't it be much better for you to go through and get a better price if you are able to.

Being effective at manipulation means that you can easily manipulate companies to give you the best in deals for services and products. By promising them your praise and services, for example, you can essentially get them in the palm of your hand. They become far more willing to communicate with their managers and negotiate the best possible deal for you so that you will actively buy from them. Salespeople, especially those who are based on commission, are always eager to close a deal. This allows you to use manipulation in order to get the deal to close in your favor.

Leading the Desired Lifestyle That You Want

Each person has a goal about the desired lifestyle that they would like to have—but the lifestyle that you have right now, and the one that you desire, might not always be the same thing. However, the good thing about using manipulation is that you are able to use it to help you get to the desired lifestyle. There are a lot of ways that you can do this—you just need to learn how to make it work.

Let's say that right now you are living in a house that you are renting, and you want to buy your own home at some point—but right now, the types of homes that you are the most interested in purchasing are not within the price that you can purchase. However, with the right kind of manipulation, you may find that you are able to get a better deal, putting you into the home of your dreams sooner as you would like. This can work with any of the big-ticket items that you would like to purchase, such as cars.

Another way that this can work is with some of the relationships that you are in. If you are someone who would like to find a new group of friends, the friends who are going to help you reflect your new lifestyle, you may find that working with manipulation is going to help you out. You can also use the art of persuasion to convince others to become your friends and spend time with you—and from that, you will then have the friends that you need to live this new lifestyle.

Take this a step further and see how it can work with some of your intimate relationships. If this kind of relationship doesn't look like the one that you would like, then you can bring in some manipulation and see if it is possible to make the right changes towards a better relationship. If you want to have more romance, for example, you would spend some time with fancier places or people.

Getting Out of Things

Have you ever gotten into a situation where you were asked to do something, but you didn't have any want to do it? All of the time we are going to be signed up for things, or given offers, that we aren't really that interested in—and sometimes, it can feel difficult to turn these things down in a polite manner. Depending on who is asking for the favor, you may feel obligated to help them out with it.

However, once you learn how to work with manipulation a bit more, you will find that this is not as big of a problem for you anymore. You may even find that this is a good place to start when it comes to practicing your manipulation. You can bring it up any time that you get stuck doing something that you would rather not be doing.

Not only are you able to use manipulation for your benefit to get out of the reunions or things that family and friends want you to help out with, but you can also use it at work as well. If your boss went and signed you up for something that you don't want to do, you can use manipulation to convince them to let you get out of it, or you can convince someone else to go and do the work for you.

You can use manipulation in any manner that you would like to make sure that you are able to live the life that you want. It can help you to get the business negotiations to work the way that you want, to help you get the friendships, relationships, and to get yourself out of the things that you don't want to do. There are just so many different things that you are able to use manipulation with, and this can be a great way to ensure that you have the life that you have always dreamed about.

Chapter 12　Subliminal Psychology

"On the unconscious level, touch seems to impart a subliminal sense of caring and connection" - Leonard Mlodinow

How to Influence Others

This can be easily done through brainwashing. Brainwashing relates to the temporary method of exchanging the thoughts of an individual on culture and faith with fresh concepts designed to fit the brainwashing objective. In both broader and smaller environments, brainwashing can happen. For example, a brainwasher is able to control a particular person or to control the thoughts of a broader group at once using the same techniques and principles. Brainwashing is the method by which atheists become nationalists and suicide terrorists. It is demonstrated to be efficient in nearly any situation, evaluated and demonstrated over the years.

So, what are the most prevalent brainwashing misunderstandings? Many individuals see the method as a rapid and compulsory event. Figure either Alex in "A Clockwork Orange" or Neo in "The Matrix" which unintentionally compelled concept into its cranium within a brief moment. That's brainwashing in Hollywood, and it's far from what happens in actual existence.

This section will examine in depth the method of real-world brainwashing, but brainwashing is in its entirety, the rapid, gradual, and seemingly willing change of the' chart of truth' of a person from the one voluntarily created by the brainwasher to the one imposed upon it. The malicious irony of the method is that the brainwasher ensures that the person is always in command.

The Analysis

Many individuals would share that "cults brainwashing individuals," although very few could clarify just what cults are and how their followers are brainwashing. Let the method be demystified. A cult is a set of fringes often constructed around a charismatic leader, who can affect his supporters highly. The cultivation generally gives those who pursue a "comprehensive knowledge of truth. " Why does this cultivation background precisely flourish in which brainwashing?

The main appeal of cults, if the individual is prepared to carry on the doctrines of a cult, is to show a truth as something easy and within grasp of the average person. We reside in a contemporary and complicated environment where lives can be overwhelming and messy. Cultures break through this confusion and say, "We have the response, don't care. " The manner this "answer" is displayed is designed to satisfy the natural need for membership and recognition. The concept of a "fresh ordinary" can lead to the development of brainwashing in this sense. What is "fresh ordinary" precisely? It is an influencing manner in which cult can affect people, by creating them seem predominant, recognized and beneficial, in their brainwashing. For instance, it would be extremely odd in daily existence to worship a guy that says to be God. However, this behavior becomes "normal" in the closed environment of a cult to the extent that it would not appear unusual to people within a cultic environment! This method of constant personal strengthening is one of the strongest forms of ideological cult brainwashing.

The Manipulation

We will speak about manipulative behaviors, perceptions, or topics of other people through violence, frustration, or superior strategies, as a psychological manipulation that is a social influence. The manipulator will operate to support its own objectives, generally at the cost of others, in order for most of its techniques to be regarded as fraud, frustration, and violence. Although not always adverse social influence, it can damage you when you are influenced by someone or a band. Social impact is generally considered benign, for instance when a physician operates to convince his clients to start to follow good practices. This relates to any cultural impact that is prepared to uphold the freedom of choice and not unreasonably coercive. On the other side, if anyone attempts to follow his own route and utilizes individuals against his own will, the personal consequences can be detrimental and are generally seen as adverse. Psychologist or emotional manipulation is seen as a type of manipulation and coercion. This type of intellectual command can include many elements such as bullying and brainwashing. This is usually regarded as false or abusive. Those who decide to manipulate will attempt to check their conduct. A manipulator will have some ultimate objective in mind and will operate to push the manipulator to attain the end objective by using several types of violence. Emotional hunting is often involved. The manipulators will employ mental power, brainwashing or intimidation to get others to do their job.

Perhaps the manipulator does not wish to do the job but feels that they have no option owing to challenging or other methods. Manipulative individual's absence the proper focus and sensitivity for others to avoid problems in their behavior. Other manipulators simply want to achieve the final objective and don't care about who was upset or harmed. In addition, manipulative people often fear a healthy relationship because they fear others won't embrace it. Manipulative people are often unable to recognize them. Someone with a manipulative personality cannot often bear responsibility for his own behaviors, issues, and life. As these problems cannot be taken into account, the manager utilizes manipulative techniques to carry accountability for another person. Manipulators can usually use the same approach to affect others as other mental controls. Emotional hunting is one of the most common strategies.

The handler works here to stimulate empathy or guilt on the topic he controls. These are the two feelings selected because they are the two biggest of all natural feelings. Then the manipulator is able to use his sympathy or guilt to force others to coexist or to help them achieve their final objective. Not only can the manipulator create those feelings, but it can also stimulate a degree of compassion or guilt that is far away.

This implies you can bring a scenario that does not appear to be a funeral or something that is really crucial like losing a group. Only one of the methods of manipulators is emotional punishment. One of the other stuff many manipulators succeeded was to use a type of violence called insanity. Usually, this strategy is designed to generate self-doubt in a controlled topic. This self-doubt often becomes so powerful that some may think crazy. The manipulator sometimes utilizes types of active violence to produce folly. They may also choose to convey verbal assistance or consent, but then offer non-verbal hints which differ. Often, the supervisor continually tries to undermine certain occurrences or complications while demonstrating assistance for the same behavior. You will use rejection, reasoning, rationalization, and disapproval of the evil purpose to escape the problem when you get captured in the law. One of the biggest problems with psychological manipulators is that they cannot always realize what others need. However, they are not excused for their behavior. Often, others ' demands are not seen as priorities, or the manipulator does not prioritize them to undertake manipulative activities without feeling justified or shameful. This could make it hard to prevent the conduct and clarify why the manipulator has to continue wisely. In addition, the manipulator can find it difficult to form meaningful and lasting relationships because the people they are accustomed to and have difficulty relying on the manipulator. The difficulty is informing relations in both directions, whereas the manipulator cannot recognize the needs of another person, and the other person cannot establish mental relationships or confidence in the manipulator.

The Persuasion

Many distinct responses are often discovered when individuals believe in persuasion. Some individuals might believe in ads and publicity that encourage you to buy some item over another. Others may believe in politically persuasive and how applicants can attempt to affect the opinions of the electorate to participate again. These are two instances of convincing because the signal is aimed at changing the manner the topic believes. Persuasion is a powerful power in the topic and in culture, but a huge impact. It can be discovered in everyday life. The manner persuasion functions will influence the press, the advertising, legal decision-making, and politics. As this manual illustrates, there are significant distinctions between persuasive individuals and other types of command. In the context of brainwashing and hypnosis, the topic is isolated to alter its mind and personality.

Manipulation works to attain the supreme objective for one person too. While only one topic can be compelling to alter their minds, persuasion can be applied to a broader extent to convince a whole community or community to alter its mode of thought. The ability to shift many people's minds at once can render them more efficient and perhaps more harmful, instead of just one topic.

Many people think wrong that they are exempt from convincing impacts. In your opinion, you could see every pitch of revenues whether the officer is selling a commodity or a fresh concept, then get to the point and conclude with his own logic. In several scenarios, none of the people will want to hear anything they use logic every time, especially when it is totally contrary to their belief, regardless of the strength of the argument. Most people can prevent wonderful vehicle buys or the recent item on the industry from buying television and other products. The exercise of manipulation is often subtler and it can be harder for the topic to convey its own opinions on what it is advised to do. When the deed of persuasion arrives, only the bulk will look it in an adverse context. You believe of a salesperson or colleague who is looking for adverse reflection. They believe of a merchant or a friend who is trying to convince them to alter all their convictions, which will press and trouble them until the shift happens. Although this is definitely a manner to think about motivation, often positive rather than negative can be used. For instance, public service rallies can encourage individuals to prevent smoking or recycling that can enhance the life of the individual. In the persuasion method, everything is used.

Secret Manipulation Techniques

Creating an Illusion

The manipulator will be an expert in creating illusions that will more effectively achieve its final aim. You will work out an image you want and then convince the subject that this illusion is a reality, whether it's the manipulator or not. To do so, the manipulator builds the evidence necessary to demonstrate the point that works towards its goal. In order to begin the illusion, the manipulator will put the ideas and evidence into the subject's minds. Once these ideas are in place, the manipulator can step back for a couple of days and allow for manipulation to take place in the minds of subjects. The manipulator will then have a greater chance of getting the subject on board. Manipulation is a form of mind control that the subject has difficulty avoiding.

Brainwashing and hypnosis, manipulation is capable of occurring in daily life, and it may occur in some cases without much knowledge or control over the subject. The manipulator will work discreetly to achieve their ultimate goal without suspiciousness and the process derailing. The manipulator will not worry about who they hurt or how others feel, and most will not be able to understand their subjects ' needs. You just know that you want something and the subject you have chosen will help you to achieve your goal. The techniques discussed in this chapter are intended to help explain what happens during the manipulation process and how the mind of the manipulator works during the manipulation process. It is often best to try to keep anyone who is a manipulator clear so that you can avoid this kind of intellectual control.

Lying

There are various kinds of lies that the manipulator can use to help them achieve their final goals. First of all, they say lies, and others omit parts of the truth from their subjects. It's because, if the manipulator lies, they are aware that the lie goes far better than the truth to advance their agenda. Saying the truth to someone might not help the manipulator, and it would be against its plans completely. The manipulator will say a lie rather than persuade the subject to do something for them, and it is too late to resolve the problem when the subject finds out about the lie. In the stories they tell, the manipulator might also choose to omit part of the truth. They tell parts of the truth with this method, but they keep things out which are unpleasant or which may impede progress from keeping certain things unpleasant or preventing progress. Such mentions can be just as dangerous because what the truth of the story is and what the lies are will become more and more difficult. It is important to realize that anything you say can be a lie when dealing with the manipulator. The manipulator says nothing because he just tries to abuse and use his subjects to reach that end goal. It's not a good idea to trust anything. The manipulator will do everything he can, even lying, to get what he wants and he won't be sorry about it. As long as you get what you want, you don't care too much about how this or other things affect you.

Putting Another Person Down

If the manipulator uses verbal know-how to dismantle his subject, he/she risks making the subject feel as if he/she is attacked personally. When the subject feels attacked, he or she will blow and will not support the manipulator as he or she wishes. Rather, the manipulator won't like the subject and will remain as far away as possible, making it very hard for the manipulator to meet his ultimate objective. This is why the manipulator won't just walk around and talk about it. You must be discerning about the process and find a way to do it. You need to be more discerning about the process and find a way to achieve this without elevating red flags or feeling that the subject is being attacked. One way to do this is with humor. Humor can reduce barriers otherwise because humor is funny and makes people feel great. The manipulator can make his insult a joke. Although the plain has become a joke, it works just as effectively as if the joke wasn't there without leaving the visible scars. The manipulator often turns its position into a third person. This helps them more easily mask what they say and provides an easy way to deny the harm if they come back later to haunt them. If you are still able to guess the comments are made on them, you might start putting them down with "other people think. . . " if the subject is able to guess, then the manipulator will end with a lift line which may include something like "present company except, of course. "   It elevates the manipulator to a new level and makes it feel that something is desirable. The topic is more likely to improve things and fix any mistakes they have made. This puts the manipulator in a position of power and makes it easier for them to help.

Techniques of Deception

Equivocations

This is if contradictory, ambiguous, or indirect statements are made by the agent. This is to confuse the subject and not to understand what's happening. It can also help the agent to protect himself if the subject returns and tries to attribute the wrong information to them.

Concealments

It's one of the most frequently used types of deceit. Obstacles are when the agent intentionally or intentionally omits information which is relevant, relevant, or relevant to the context or involves any behavior that would conceal information relevant to the subject in this specific context. The agent will not have linked the subject directly, but he or she will ensure that the important information needed is never relevant

Exaggerations

That is when an agent over-emphasizes a fact or extends the truth a bit so that the story becomes the way they want. While the agent may not lie straight to the issue, it will make the situation look bigger than it really is or it will change the truth a little, so the subject will do what it wants.

Understatements

An understatement is the exact opposite of the overstatement tool because it will play down or minimize the truth aspects. You will say that an event is not so much when, in fact, it could be the thing which will determine whether the subject is graduated or promoted. Later on, the agent can say how it did not understand the size of a deal, so it looks good, and the subject looks almost small if they complain.

Chapter 13   Manipulation In Relationship

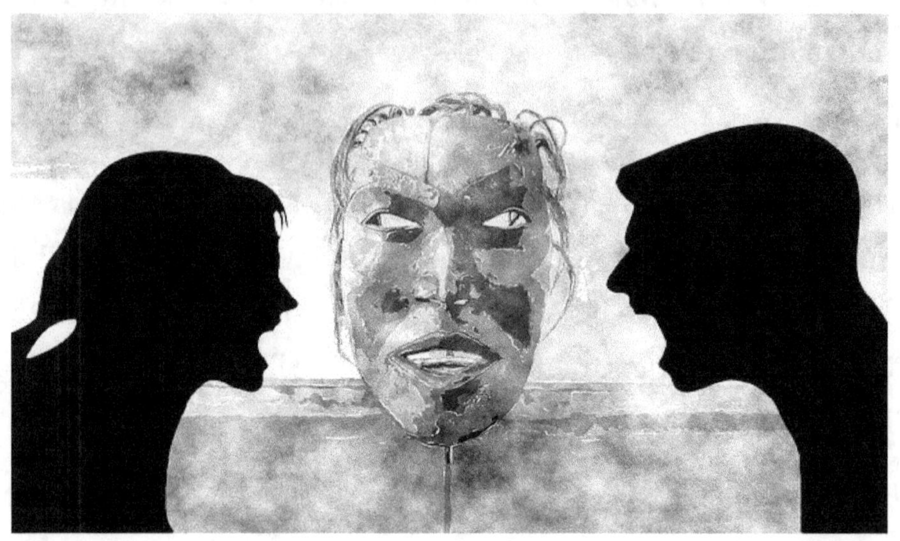

"We can improve our relationships with others by leaps and bounds if we become encouragers instead of critics"
- Joyce Meyer

The first year of their relationship was perfect. Barrett was everything Susan had ever dreamed of. They went on vacations and Barrett even went to Thanksgiving at Susan's parents. After that first year came to an end, things start to change. Barrett started to demand things from Susan. He stopped giving you any attention, he asked for money and used her house to throw parties. If Susan refused to give him something, Barrett fought and would ignore her for days. All Susan wanted was the good days during their first year, so she tried everything to make sure Barrett was happy.

After two more years of the relationship, Susan eventually realized that Barrett was controlling her life.

Manipulation in relationships is a big issue for many, and it doesn't happen in just romantic relationships. Family members or friends have the ability to control and twist a person's emotions. You are stuck living in the false hope of reaching perfect relationships with them. This is why it takes so long for a person to realize they are being manipulated.

Manipulation in Romantic Relationships

Out definition of manipulation referred to deliberate acts to control people. However, when it comes to romantic relationships, people will sometimes manipulate each other unintentionally as well. Whether conscious or not, it is still toxic and for a person's life and mind.

1.   How are you living your life?

Do you live yours or theirs? A romantic relationship is about sharing each other's life. Manipulative partners bring you into theirs and make you disconnect from your own. Think about this:

•   If you are friends with your partner's, is your partner friends with yours?

•   How often do you go out to your favorite places?

- Did you move into their house or apartment?

When they bring you into their surroundings, they can control you more easily. Since you aren't comfortable within those surroundings, you do things according to the will of your partner.

When you are in a new relationship, you may not know for certain if they are manipulating you, or just shy about sharing your life. This means you need to test them. Make the relationship 50/50. Share parts of their life, but also encourage them to do things that you like. Let them know that you are committed to the relationship if it remains healthy and equal.

1.   Do you do things because you're nice?

How often does your partner talk you into doing something because they say something like, "Your kind, so you'll understand."

When it comes to protecting yourself from being taken advantage of because of your sensitivities, you have to remind yourself that you aren't a bad person just because you tell your partner no. Then, try to come up with a reasonable alternative. For example, if they expect you to give them money for something to prove your love, say, "My money and love are two different things. You know I would help if I could." This keeps your sensitivities from clouding your decision.

1.   Are you the butt of the joke?

Manipulative partners are often hurtful jokers. If you get upset, they say something like, "I was just kidding. Quit being so sensitive." They make you feel like you're overreacting to something meaningless, but this is very manipulative. When they do this in public, it aids in their control over you. You can't react to the things they say when it is in public because then you will look like the bad guy.

This also works in private. They attack your insecurities to win an argument or control what you are doing.

In this situation, you have to stand up for yourself. No matter how funny their statement may have been, you need to call it out. Don't be as rude as them, but make sure they understand that you don't appreciate what you said.

You can say something like, "Please don't say things like that again. I don't think it's funny."

You can also say, "Are you trying to upset me... Then quit saying things like that."

If you are able to shut them down as soon as they say something, they will be less likely to say things like that in the future.

Family Manipulation

It hurts when you realize your family has been manipulating you. Manipulation is common in a romantic relationship, but people usually skip over manipulation at the hands of sisters, brothers, mothers, and fathers.

When you have a family member who has a manipulative nature and a false sense of pride will try to control their home as if it is their kingdom. Families then become instruments for the manipulator.

It's hard to understand family manipulation because you grew up with these people. You are conditioned for their behavior, so you find it hard to realize you are being manipulated.

1.   Is there anybody that acts very selfless?

There are plenty of honorable family members, but then there are some who imitate these caring family members. Selflessness is an act manipulator use. They say things like, "Have I ever done anything just for myself?" The main difference between the real selfless person and the manipulator is that the manipulator will gladly remind you of everything that they have ever done.

In situations like these, you must realize that people who praise their own selfless acts aren't truly selfless. You can respond to them by saying, "I appreciate the things you have done for the family, but I am old enough to make my own decisions."

1.   Do you ever get shamed?

Family members have front row access to your weaknesses. Good family members help to protect them, but manipulative people use them to bully you and cause you to feel shameful. It is common for them to use shame to blackmail or control you.

It's important to build up your self-esteem. They work on your insecurities, so try to overcome them. Then the manipulator won't have anything to play with. Keep in mind that everybody has a weakness.

Friendship Manipulation

One-sided friendships are a common occurrence. You get asked to do things for them, but if you ask them out to do something, they are always busy. Some friends find it fun to control others. This typically starts during school and goes with them through life.

1.   Is your friend trying to control you?

The manipulative friend wants to make sure that you follow their ideas. You feel like they control everything whenever you are around them. They may even try to control how you dress, your decisions, and other relationships. They act as a guide, but they just like exploiting your vulnerability.

Start looking to see how many times your friend questions what you do and say and then tries to push you towards their point of view. If you start noticing clear signs, stand up for yourself. Say something like, "I can make my own decisions."

1. Does your friend ignore you?

Conversations with a manipulative friend don't mean anything. They don't really care about you. If they don't find what you are saying is interesting, they will stop listening. You have to realize that they have little to no concern for what is going on in your life. Call them out if you have to. Say something like, "I am trying to tell you something. I would appreciate it if you would focus on me or just tell me that you are not interested." This keeps them from taking you for granted.

1. Is your friend always "busy" when you need them?

Manipulative friends show up when they need something. Once that's taken care of, they disappear. When you try to get in touch with them for something, they are busy. If the friendship works this way, you never see them unless they need you, then they aren't really your friend. It's best to cut ties with them and stop giving them any attention.

Chapter 14　Personal Benefit Of Mind Control And Manipulation

"No matter what you do, your person comes through. You can't completely change yourself on the screen. I had in mind someone colder and more in control, but I couldn't do it. This human note just crept in and maybe it's better" - Leslie Caron

While we often think of manipulation as a bad thing, but there are actually quite a few benefits that are going to come with using manipulation in order to get what we want.

Just because we are getting what we want doesn't mean that we are going to always harm someone else. And this is the difference between regular manipulation and what is known as dark manipulation. It is an important distinction that we need to make. With regular manipulation, we want to get something, but we don't want the other person to get harmed or hurt in any manner, whether it is physical, mental, or emotional.

On the other hand, when it comes to dark manipulation, it isn't going to matter to the manipulator whether the other person gets harmed or not. They don't really care how much that person is harmed, and usually, there is going to be some kind of harm in the process. As long as the manipulator gets the thing that they want, they are going to be happy about the situation.

With that said, whether you are using manipulation in order to progress your own agenda while helping others (like in sales or getting some help on a group project), or you are using it to benefit yourself and you don't care if someone gets harmed in the process, there are going to be some benefits that come with using manipulation on a regular basis. Some of the benefits you can look for will include:

Manipulation is often going to work. The idea here is that if I know what I want and I know how to evoke a feeling in the other person so that they are more likely to do what I want, then manipulation is going to be effective, and we are able to measure this effect as well. Think of how this works. Businesses are going to spend billions of dollars in research to do various marketing strategies to point to how well the manipulation that is found in their campaigns and their advertisements work, so we know that manipulation must be something that works.

Of course, you have to do things the right way. it is not enough to just put an ad online or on television and assume people are going to come in droves to purchase the product. There is just too much competition out there, and often we see so many advertisements that it is impossible to just see something and be manipulated by it. There has to be another level, and there needs to be some experience and expertise to pull it off, and that is what the research dollars of many companies are spending on.

The same idea can be said when we take a look at regular manipulation that an individual is going to use. It is not enough for us to walk up to someone and say, "Do what I want!" The target is likely going to take a look at us and just laugh and walk away. And you would do the same as well. You need to make sure that you are using the right techniques, and that you really understand what the other person will respond to. When you use manipulation in the right manner though, and with the right techniques you will find that it actually works which is a really cool benefit.

The next benefit that comes with manipulation is the idea that we can become pretty good at it. In fact, as you went over the previous chapter, it is likely that you saw at least a few times when you have used manipulation in the past to help you get what you wanted, even if the answers ended up surprising you in the process. This manipulation is actually something that we have been practicing since before we were able to walk.

This is because there was a time when we were not able to talk, and we still needed to get things. We needed food something to drink to feel loved to have clothes, to get baths to get diapers changed and more. Even though we were not able to talk and voice our opinions on our own, and we were not able to take care of these things on own at this time, we were able to use manipulation in order to influence mom and dad to do the work for us.

Since we have been able to read others since a young age in order to help us get what we wanted as a baby up through adulthood, we are already good at reading others, often much better than we would think. And we can even find that, with a bit of practice, we are able to quickly guess the right thing to do to help us motivate that other person in the process as well. Of course, some of us are going to be much better at doing this than others, but it is still something that we can work on to improve and see some great results with influencing others.

Easier to get what we want. If you decided to come right out and ask the other person to give you exactly what you wanted, it is likely that they are going to say no. if you just ask about it, without using any of the techniques that we will discuss in this guidebook and the techniques of manipulation, then the other person really has no need to help you and won't feel guilty about doing something that they have no interest in helping out with.

However, if you are able to use some of the manipulation tools and techniques that we have been discussing so far, and you are able to trigger some feelings in the other person, you will find that it is easier to get the other person to do what you want. They are going to feel some kind of obligation in order to help you, even if they are not sure what that is all about. And even if they are not fond of the idea of helping out with it, they are more likely to say yes.

This is going to be really great news for you. It means that you are going to be able to get the other person to say yes to what you want them to, without having to push too hard or worry as much about whether they are going to say yes or no to you. You will have already put in the work that is needed to convince them to work with you, and it is likely, especially if you spent time analyzing them and using the right technique for their needs, that they are going to agree to what you want.

And the final benefit that we are going to take a look at here when it comes to using manipulation and some of the different techniques that come with it is the idea of power. Since all relationships whether they are with family, at work, or an intimate relationship, are going to have some element of power in them. All of us would like to have power over others or at least over someone at some point, and manipulation is going to be the tool that we need to ensure that we gain that power over our target.

Now, there are those who will take that power and go too far. This is where the manipulation is going to turn into abuse and some other problems as well. But the power that comes with manipulation can sometimes be as simple as having a bit of control over one person in your life, even your child, and it doesn't always have to be an abusive or negative kind of thing to work with.

The negatives of manipulation

Of course, there have to be a few negatives that come with manipulation. If there weren't, then everyone would use this technique all of the time and we wouldn't have some of the negative connotations that come with it along the way either. The negatives of this are going to mainly occur when you are not versed well enough in using manipulation or if someone catches you in the act of manipulating them. We will explore these a bit more as we get through these sections. Some of the different negatives that can come with using manipulation in your own life can include:

Manipulation is something that has the potential to backfire quite a bit. People are often going to have some kind of sense about when another person is trying to manipulate them. This is because we are heightened to the idea that because we want something out of another person, it is likely that someone else is going to want something out of us as well. When someone starts to sense that they are being manipulated, it is not going to end well for you and it is often going to generate a lot of anger, resentment and more.

If the target senses that the manipulator is trying to take control, or they feel that the manipulator is trying to take some power over them in a sneaky manner, it is likely that the target is not going to trust that person any longer. At this point, if the target feels like you have successfully manipulated them, they may withhold something from their manipulator in order to get even, even if it is not that big of a deal what you are trying to get. And if the target thinks that this manipulation has gone even further and feels like their feelings are being toyed with, then it is sure to bring out a big power struggle between the two people in this game, and the trust is going to head right out the window.

Another negative to be careful about is that we often are not going to think through the manipulation that we are doing before we do it. Before we even have a good idea of what we want out of the relationship, or before we start to evaluate the possibility of just coming out to the target and asking for what we want in a direct manner, we are going to head right over and start manipulating the other person.

The reason that we do this is because we are so eager to try out the techniques, we are eager to get what we want, or we just assume that the other person will say no to us and we don't want to worry about the rejection in the process. This step though is going to lead to some assumptions about you both that could end up corroding the relationship that you are in. remember that once the relationship is gone and corroded, it is impossible for you to regain the control that you need in order to manipulate that person again.

There are a lot of different indirect versions of manipulation that can come into play, and sometimes they will become almost a habit in the relationship. Some of these are going to include options like guilt tripping, abusive criticism, and complaining. And another layer of the power struggle is going to start showing up in the relationship when we use these techniques all of the time, even though that was usually not the intention.

The best way to avoid this kind of issue is to make sure that you don't jump into the manipulation too quickly. You need to be able to think it all through properly, and really consider when you will use it, how much you will use, how you will manipulate and more. Manipulation is something that has to be thought out, and if you are not ready to do that, then you are going to find that it is hard to keep control over your target.

And finally, there are some people who jump into the idea of manipulation in order to give them power, control, and everything that they imagined they ever wanted. And for some of these manipulators, that is exactly what they want and they couldn't be happier. On the other hand, there are some people who find that doing this manipulation is not going to give them what they want.

Think of it this way. Maybe you manipulated someone into a relationship with you and into saying they love you because you were looking for some attention and love from another person. You finally get into that relationship and get them to say those words. But it just isn't going to satisfy most people the way that they had hoped because they know that the other person was tricked into saying it. Yes, the target is going to say they did it on their own, but the manipulator knows the work they did behind the scenes to make those words come out. Sure, you technically got what you wanted out of the situation, but it just doesn't seem as satisfying when it is done this way.

As you can see here, there are a lot of different benefits that are going to come into play when it is time to use manipulation. And this is often why people will choose to work with manipulation in order to help them gain power, get control over someone else, and to get what they want out of life. But it is important to note that there are also going to be some negatives that come with manipulation, and it doesn't always work out the way that you would like. Understanding both sides of the story before you start to use these tools of manipulation can make a world of difference as well.

Chapter 15   10 Tips How To Deal With Manipulative People

"If you don't give education to people, it is easy to manipulate them" - Pele

Being a manipulation expert is as much about spotting manipulation and deception in others as it is about leading others to do what you want them to.

Do you want to safeguard yourself from manipulation on a daily basis?

Do you want to prevent people from taking advantage of you for fulfilling their own selfish goals?

Do you want to be able to sniff manipulation from miles away?

Here are 10 brilliant strategies to protect yourself from manipulation.

1. Ignore Their Words and Actions

Manipulators almost always go after shaking people's confidence and making them insecure to get them to do what they (the manipulators) want. They will do their best to plant seeds of apprehension and self-doubt. There is a tendency to make the victim believe that the manipulator's opinion is actually the truth or fact. Rather than wanting to help you, they are more interested in trying to control you.

The best strategy to deal with these negative manipulators is to ignore them rather than trying to argue with them or correct them. This allows them to set an even deeper trap for you. Do not fall for their conflict or confrontation bet. Simply bypass them, without revealing your emotions. Do not let them see the emotions that make you tick. Once they gain a good understanding of your emotional triggers, they will sneakily use it for influencing your thoughts, behavior, and decisions.

Some people are difficult to delete from our life immediately. Think – boss, neighbor, family member, etc. Just pretend to listen to what they are saying, agree with it and eventually do exactly what you want.

2. Do not Compromise

Guilt is one of the most insidious tools used by manipulators to get their victims to do what they want. Of course, it can be used positively to influence a person too, but in negative manipulation, its usage can spell disaster for the victim.

Manipulators induce a feeling of guilt in their victims for their past mistakes, choices, and failures. They will make you guilt about being self-assured and self-confident. Each time you experience happiness, they will make you feel bad about it. Their objective is to never make you feel good about yourself or happy.

They'll sow seeds of self-doubt about your true worth, persona, and abilities. Do not get knocked off balance or feel guilty they start blaming you. Do not doubt your self-worth or abilities. Never believe that you do not deserve happiness or to feel wonderful about yourself. Take pride in who you are and your accomplishments. Build a strong sense of self-esteem and confidence. Do not compromise on your happiness or your feelings about yourself.

3. Do not Fit In, Stand Out

It isn't funny how many people make them susceptible to manipulation by trying hard to fit in. Manipulative people count of your desire to want to fit in to push their agenda. They lead you to believe that everyone does what they want you to do and that those who do not conform are abnormal. That is the only way to control your decisions and behavior.

Give up the notion of trying to fit in, and encourage the idea of standing out among the rest. Be different from other folks. Focus on reinventing yourself, laying your own rules (for what is good for you and others) and avoid cowing down to peer pressure.

4. Stop Seeking Permission

We've been conditioned to ask for permission since childhood, right from when we wanted to be fed as a baby to when we wanted to visit the bathroom in school to waiting for our turn to talk in the boardroom. The result of this conditioning is that people seldom do anything without seeking permission.

There is an excessive focus on being polite and making things comfortable for others. Manipulative people want their victims to live by their own self-drafted, imaginary rules or values. The underlying idea is you are not free to take any decision without consultation. Be brave and give up this sense of confinement. You have the power to change your life without the need to live by someone else's self-fulfilling rules.

5. Do not be a Baby

If you are tricked once, it isn't your fault. However, if you are tricked 15 times, there's something wrong with you. Do not let people take advantage of your by being everyone's favorite punching bag. Have the courage to stand up to manipulators and say a firm no when you know they are taking advantage of you. Stop whining about other people are taking advantage of you, and take complete control of your life.

Victims of manipulation almost always complain about how people use them. No one can take advantage or you without your consent. You are indeed responsible for your own actions and their outcome. If someone has used sneaky tricks to outwit you, it is your fault. Learn from past blunders and stop trusting slippery people again and again. Move away from them. Focus on surrounding yourself with positive, constructive, inspiring and like-minded folks who make you feel good about yourself.

6. Have a Clear Sense of Purpose

When you do not know what you want, you'll be more prone to do whatever everyone else wants. You'll be easily tricked into doing what other people want you to do without a firm goal or objective in life. People who lack a clear purpose or aim tend to function or go through life more mechanically. There is little logic in their actions or decisions. They will be more prone to experiencing a growing sense of emptiness in them that will craftily be filled by a manipulator.

This lack of objective or constructive activities makes the manipulator feel empowered enough to easily distract you or draw you to their agenda.

Have a higher purpose in life. It can be anything from taking up a cause for the betterment of the community to traveling around the world to rising in your professional life. Do not allow manipulators an opportunity to prey on your sense of purposelessness. When you are absolutely clear about where you are headed, it is difficult to stop you or get you to change tracks.

Conclusion

Manipulation isn't making people do what you want them to do but to get them to do what you want them to do. But how can you get people to do what you want them to? First, you need to identify their genuine desires and reverse engineer it to achieve what you want.

The closer someone is to you, the easier it is to manipulate this person. So this means that romantic partners are the best to test the secrets of manipulation.

If you want to persuade people, you have to be ready to make people see and feel like it was their decision.

Many people want to manipulate others for short-term gain. However, the genuine art of manipulation is defined by the long game. One has to be patient. The same way professionals make their skills look easy; you need to make manipulation sound easy. But it will take time and patience to learn to execute the manipulation secrets.

One thing about the manipulation that you need to keep in mind is that you should never reveal your true intentions. Maintain your consciousness of how you are making them feel and attempt to manipulate for the best.

Lastly, the more familiar you are with manipulation tactics, the harder it will be for anyone to use them

against you. The truth is that manipulators are found everywhere, and they are everyone:

- Your boss
- Your family
- Your boyfriend or girlfriend
- Your workmates
- The media
- 99.99% of people.

It is only the techniques that vary, and now you know what they are.

The next time a person attempts to influence you, you will see it coming from a mile away, and you can either decide to ignore it, or you can choose to call them out on it.

www.ingramcontent.com/pod-product-compliance
Lightning Source LLC
Chambersburg PA
CBHW070709250726
48662CB00001B/327